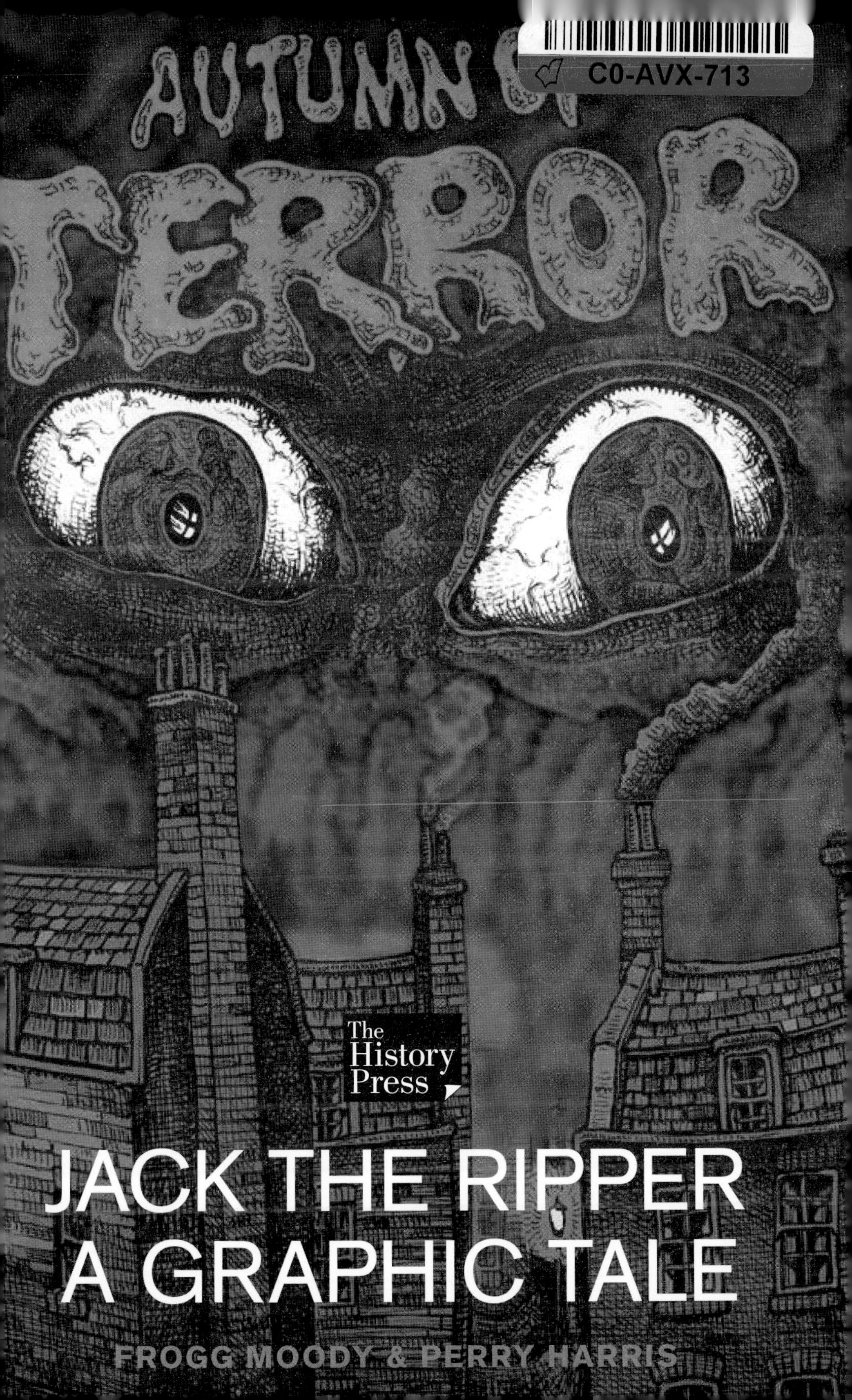
AUTUMN
TERROR
The History Press
JACK THE RIPPER
A GRAPHIC TALE
FROGG MOODY & PERRY HARRIS

First published 2014

The History Press
The Mill, Brimscombe Port
Stroud, Gloucestershire, GL5 2QG
www.thehistorypress.co.uk

British Library Cataloguing in Publication Data.
A catalogue record for this book is available from the British Library.

ISBN 978 0 7509 5453 2

Typesetting and origination by The History Press
Printed in Great Britain

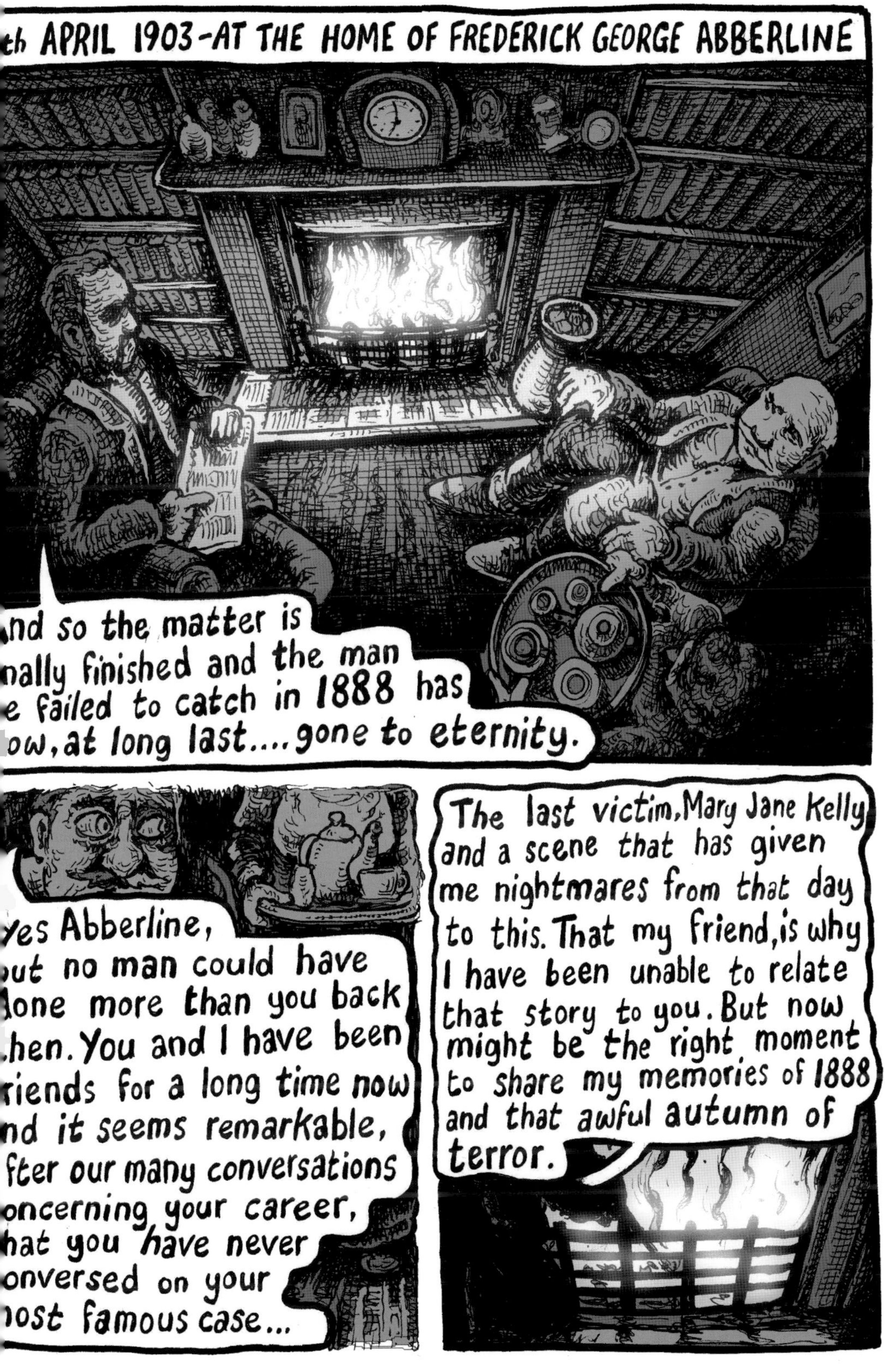
th APRIL 1903-AT THE HOME OF FREDERICK GEORGE ABBERLINE
nd so the matter is nally finished and the man e failed to catch in 1888 has ow, at long last.... gone to eternity.
yes Abberline, ut no man could have lone more than you back hen. You and I have been riends for a long time now nd it seems remarkable, fter our many conversations oncerning your career, hat you have never onversed on your ost famous case...
The last victim, Mary Jane Kelly and a scene that has given me nightmares from that day to this. That my friend, is why I have been unable to relate that story to you. But now might be the right moment to share my memories of 1888 and that awful autumn of terror.

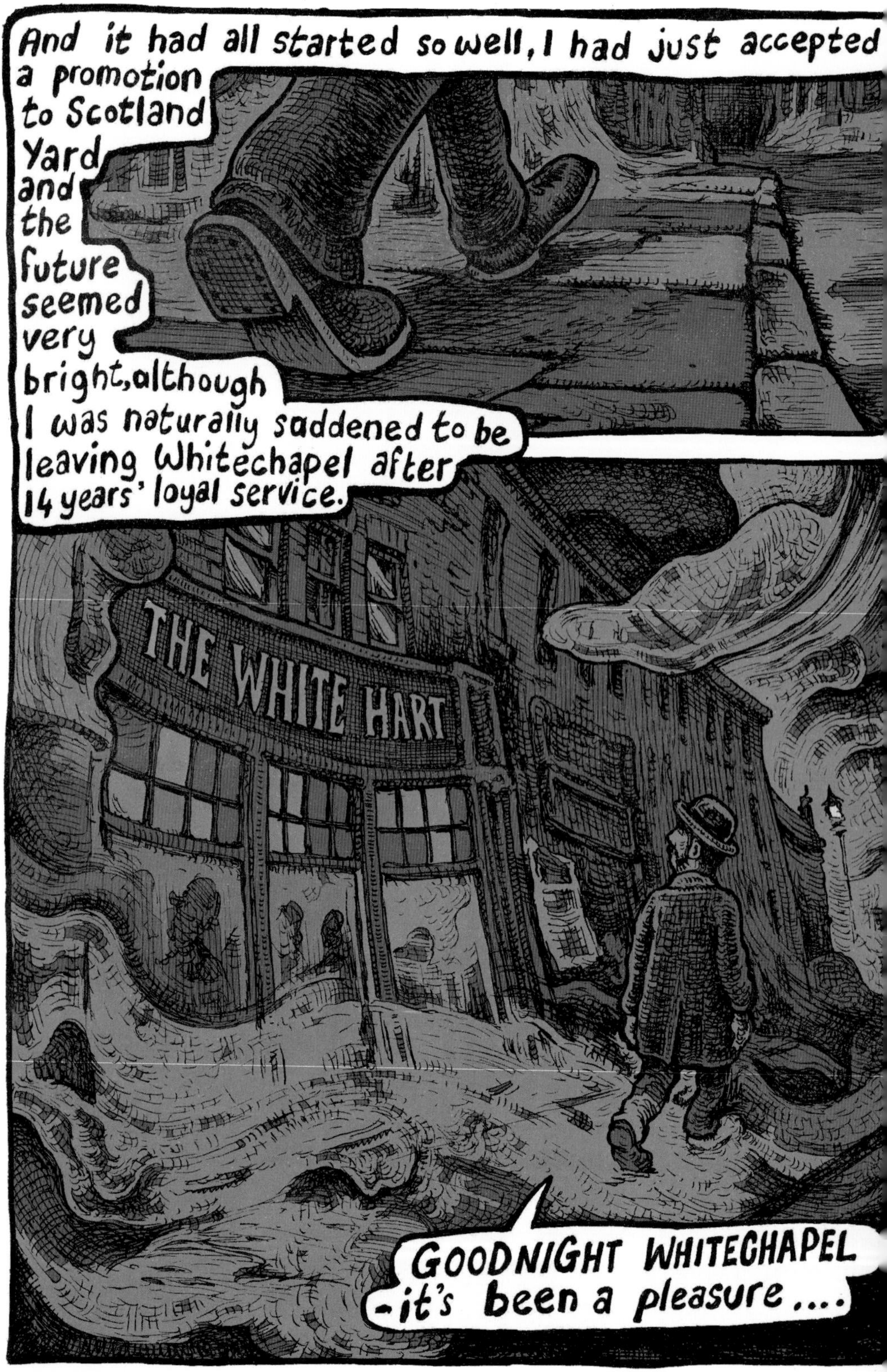
And it had all started so well, I had just accepted a promotion to Scotland Yard and the future seemed very bright, although I was naturally saddened to be leaving Whitechapel after 14 years' loyal service.
THE WHITE HART
GOODNIGHT WHITECHAPEL -it's been a pleasure ...

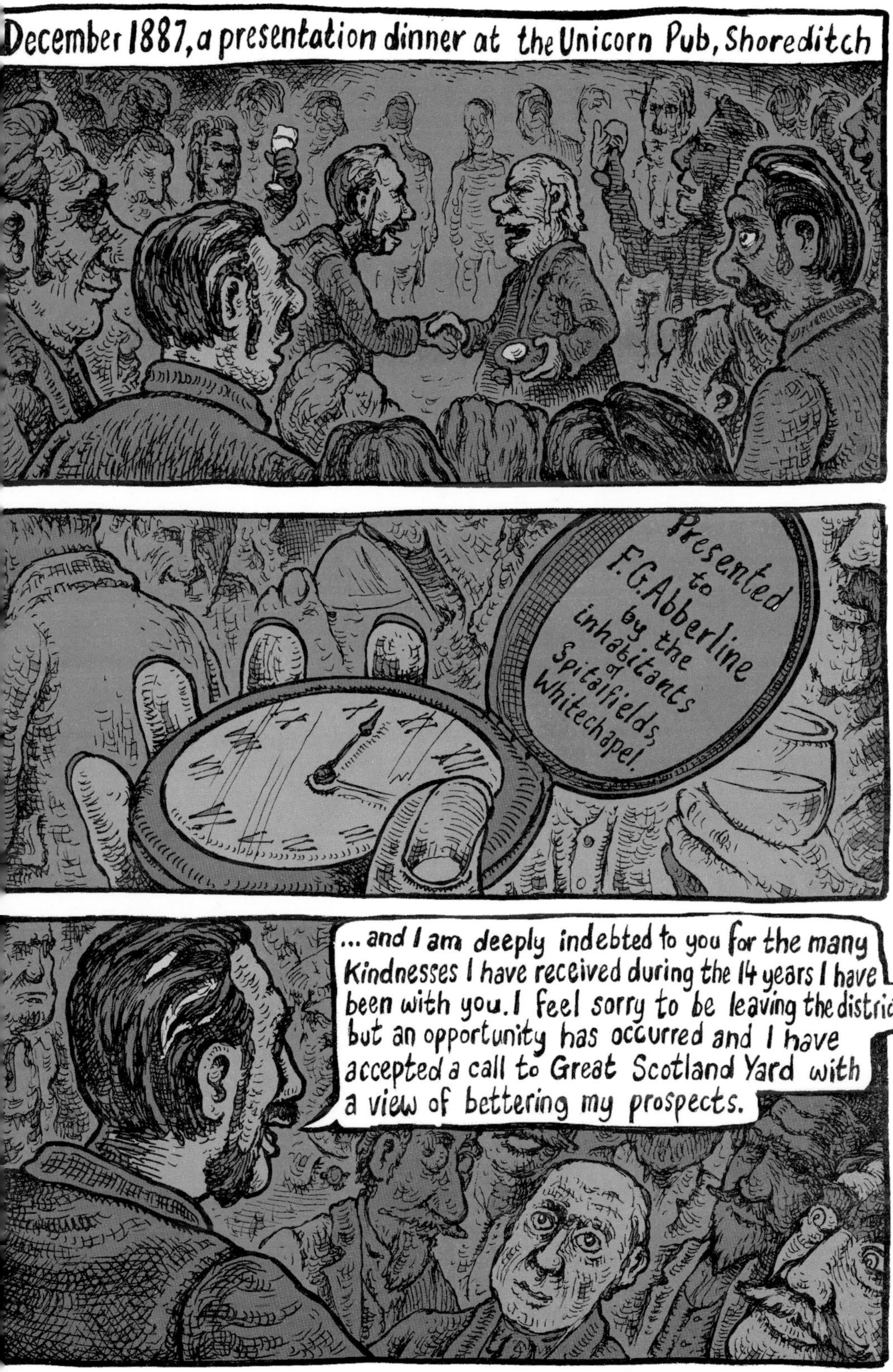
December 1887, a presentation dinner at the Unicorn Pub, Shoreditch
Presented to F.G. Abberline by the inhabitants of Spitalfields, Whitechapel
...and I am deeply indebted to you for the many Kindnesses I have received during the 14 years I have been with you. I feel sorry to be leaving the district but an opportunity has occurred and I have accepted a call to Great Scotland Yard with a view of bettering my prospects.

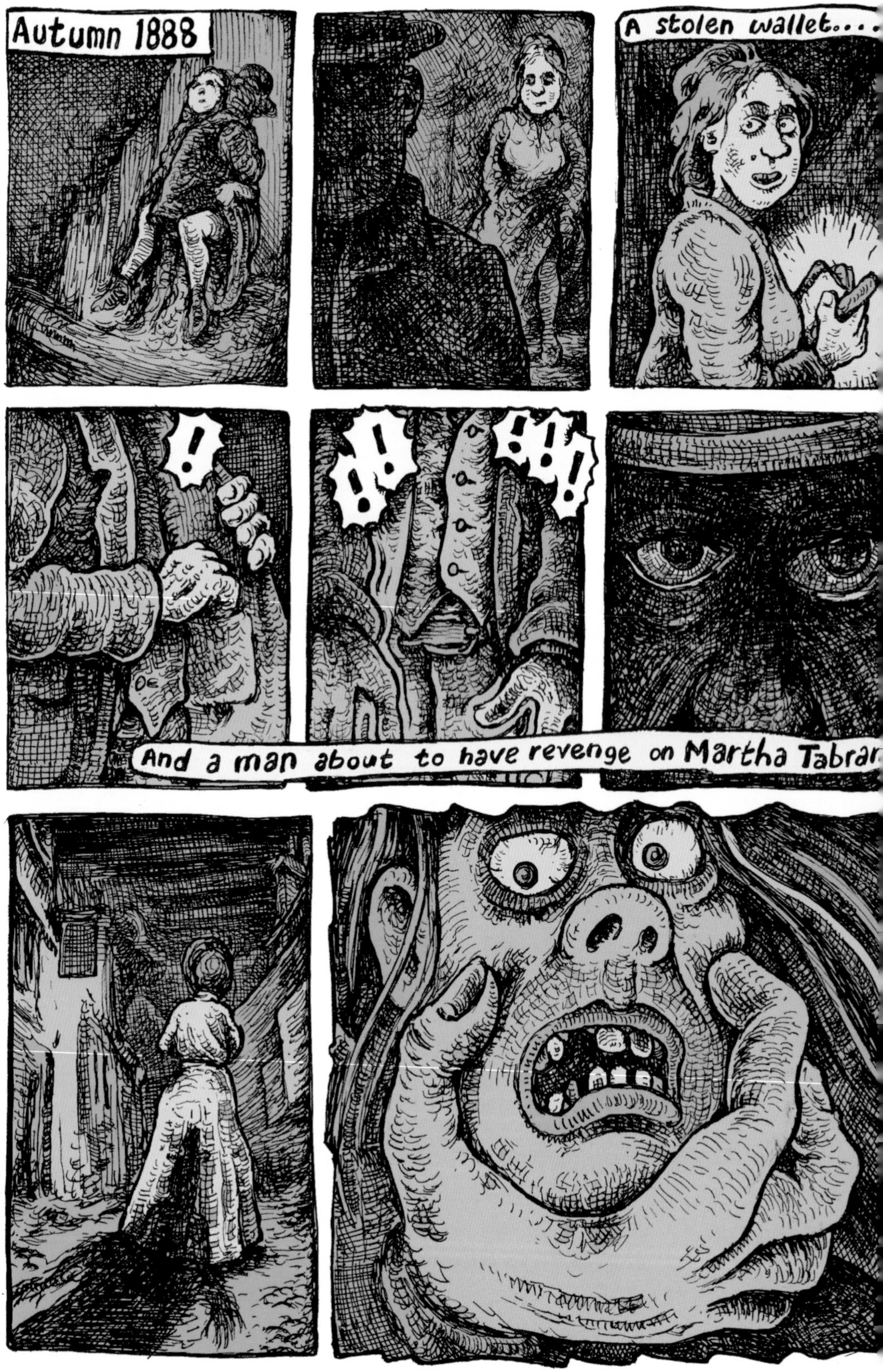
Autumn 1888
A stolen wallet....
!
!!
!!!
And a man about to have revenge on Martha Tabran

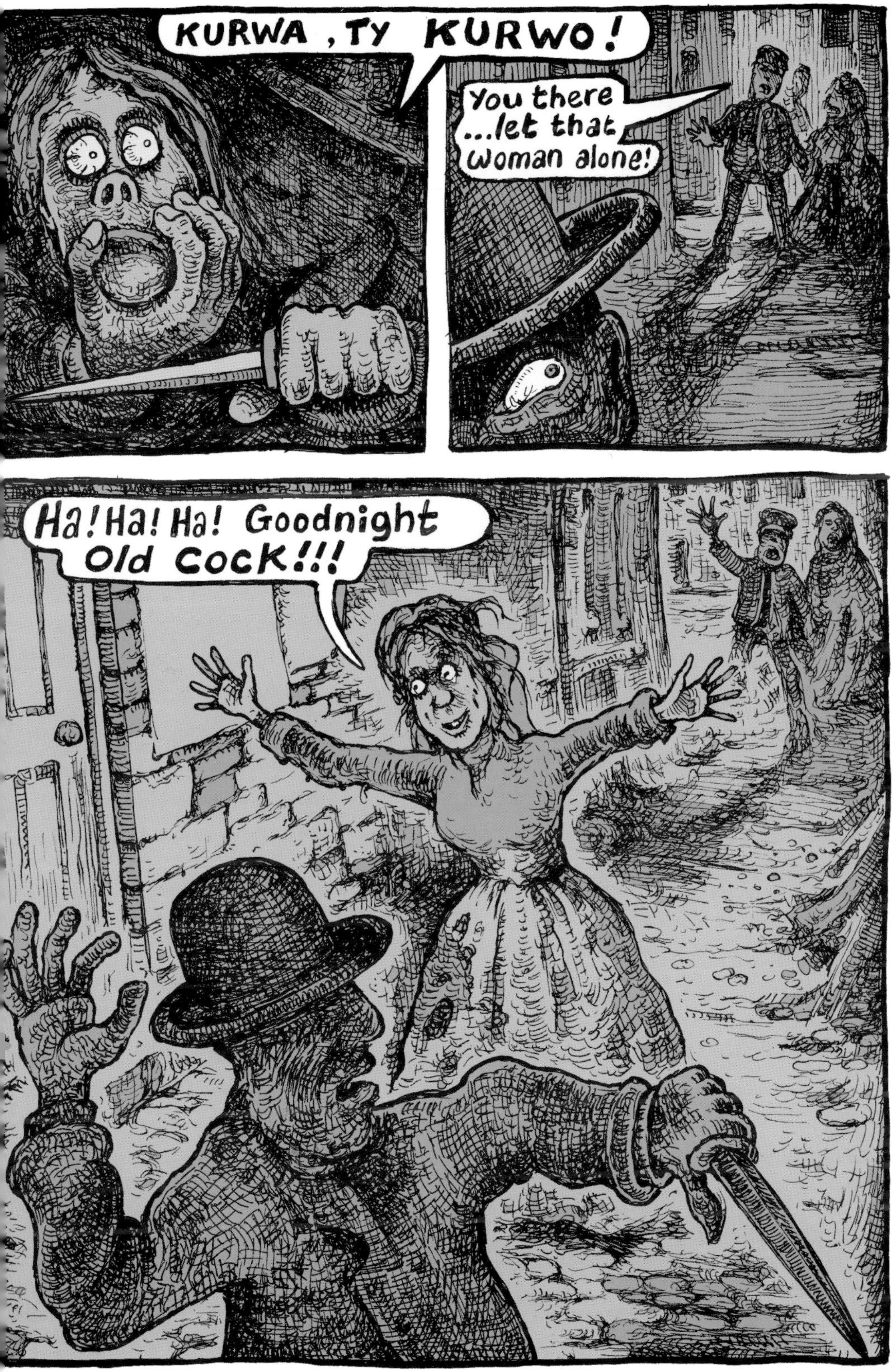
KURWA, TY KURWO!
You there ...let that woman alone!
Ha! Ha! Ha! Goodnight Old Cock!!!

SOME WEEKS LATER IN THE WHITE HART PUB, MARTHA TABRAM & PEARLY POLL OFFER THEIR SERVICES

Martha Tabram takes a soldier into George Yard buildings...

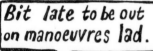

Bit late to be out on manoeuvres lad.

I'm waiting for my mate, he's gone off with a girl.

A SAVAGE ATTACK ON TABRAM BY A SOLDIER?

George Yard victim ~ pierced with **39 wounds**'

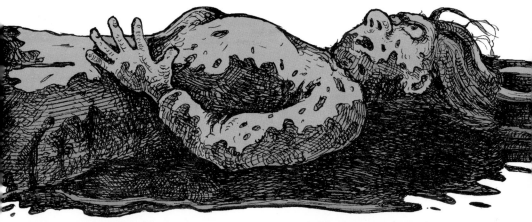

NOT A SOLDIER BUT A MAN ABOUT TO WREAK HAVOC ON LONDON'S EAST END...

John Reeve returns to George Yard buildings

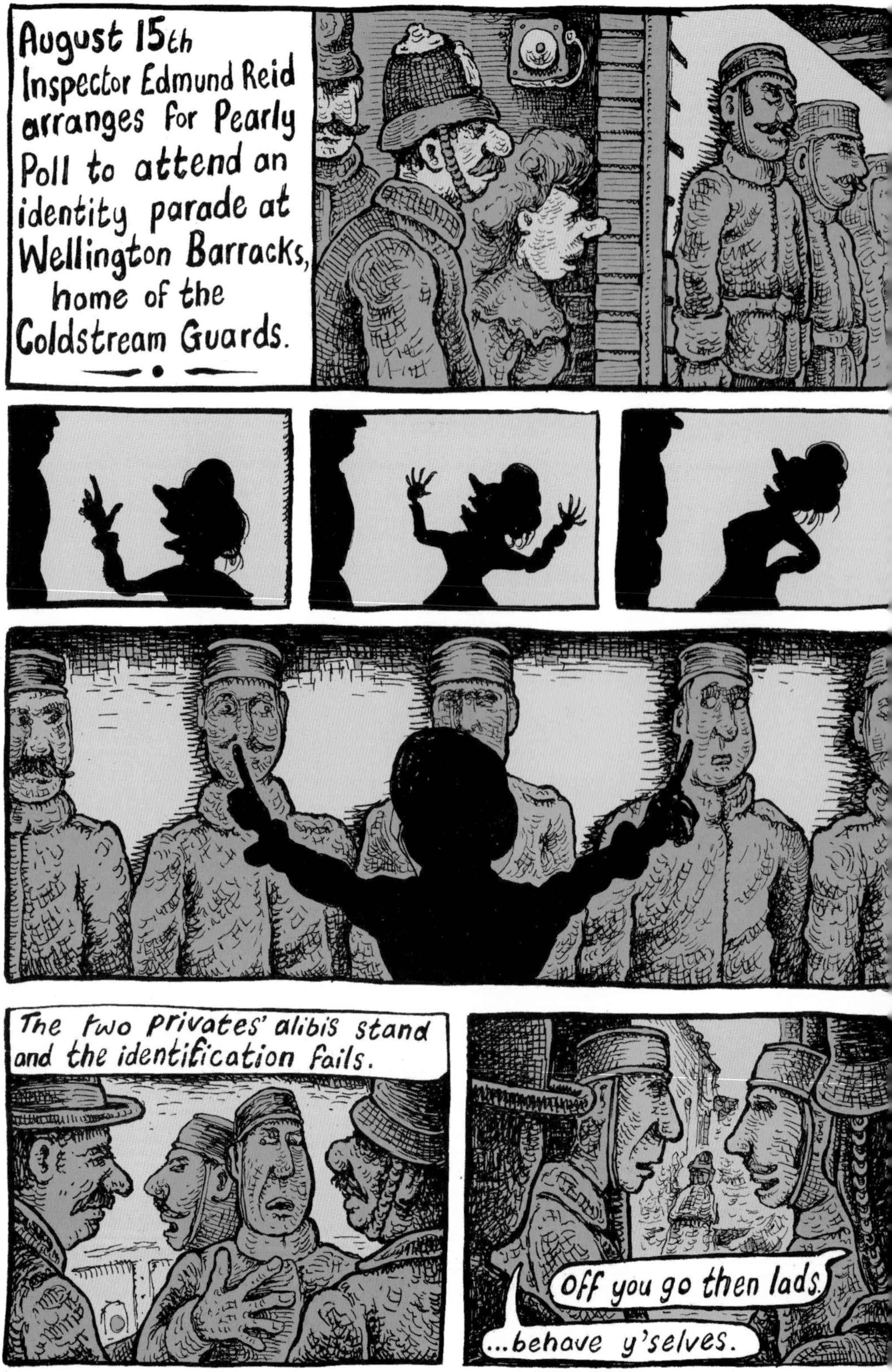

August 15th
Inspector Edmund Reid arranges for Pearly Poll to attend an identity parade at Wellington Barracks, home of the Coldstream Guards.
The two privates' alibis stand and the identification fails.
Off you go then lads.
...behave y'selves.

Tuesday August 23rd final day of the inquest at the Working Lads Institute, Inspector Reid attends. Pearly Poll is called to give evidence.

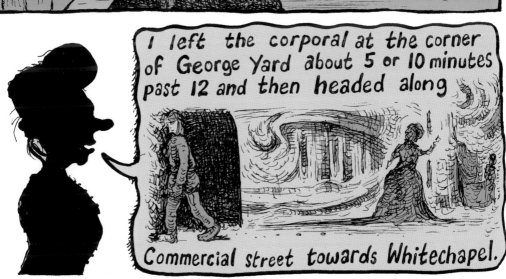

I left the corporal at the corner of George Yard about 5 or 10 minutes past 12 and then headed along Commercial street towards Whitechapel.

I heard no screams.

...was first informed of the murder on Tuesday

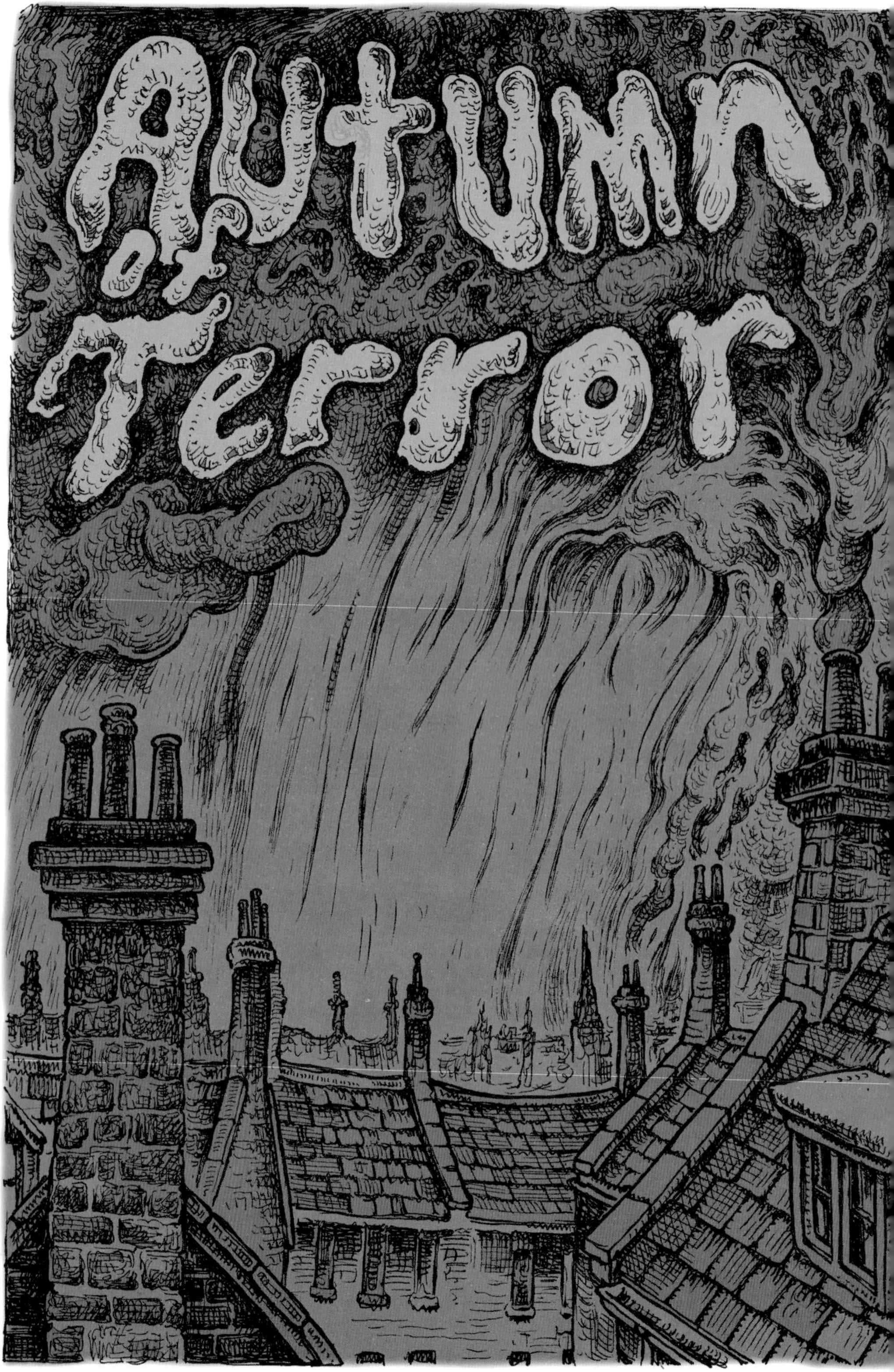
Autumn of Terror

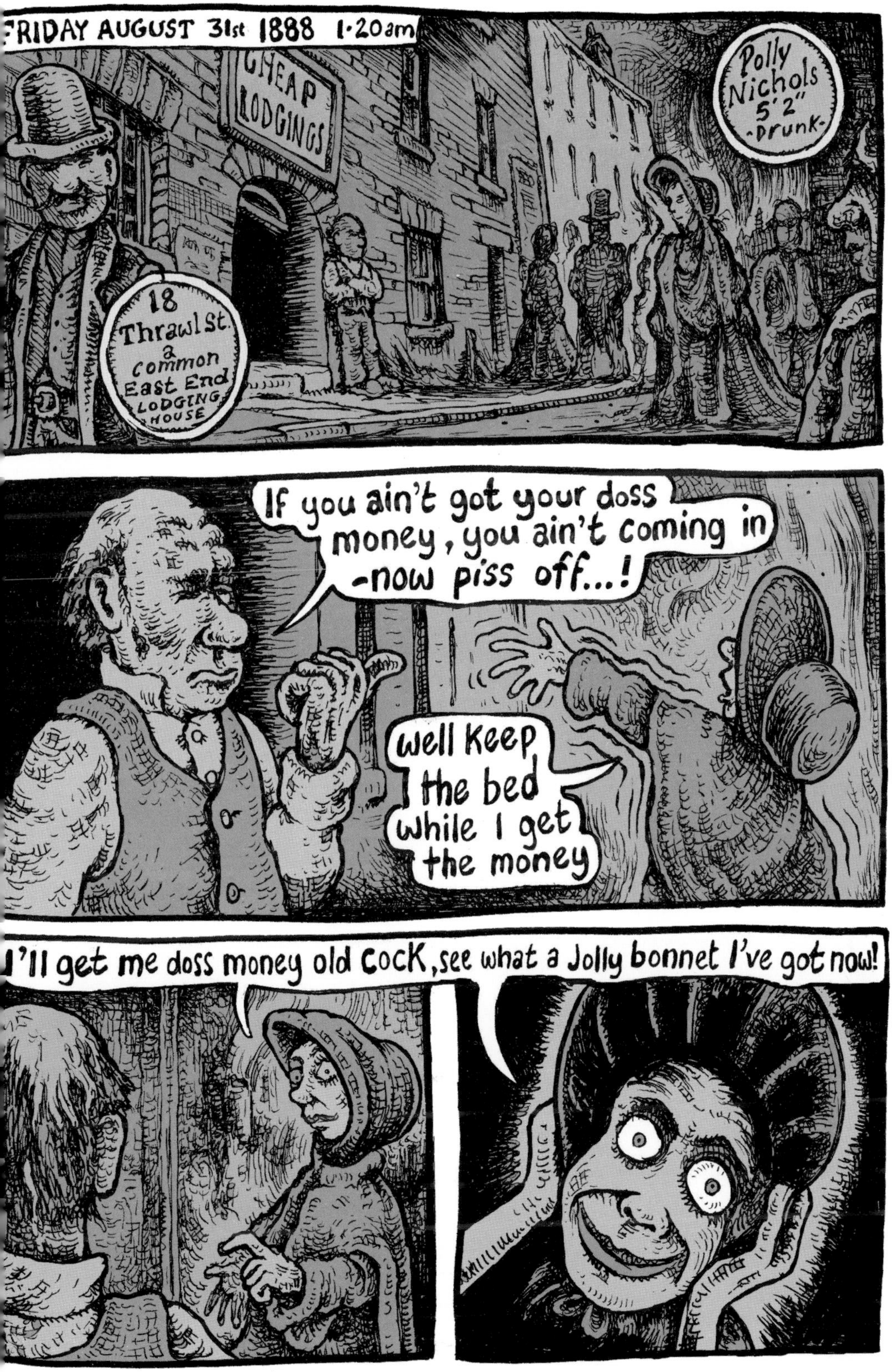
FRIDAY AUGUST 31st 1888 1·20am
CHEAP LODGINGS
Polly Nichols 5'2" -Drunk-
18 Thrawl St. a common East End LODGING HOUSE
If you ain't got your doss money, you ain't coming in -now piss off...!
well Keep the bed while I get the money
I'll get me doss money old cock, see what a Jolly bonnet I've got now!

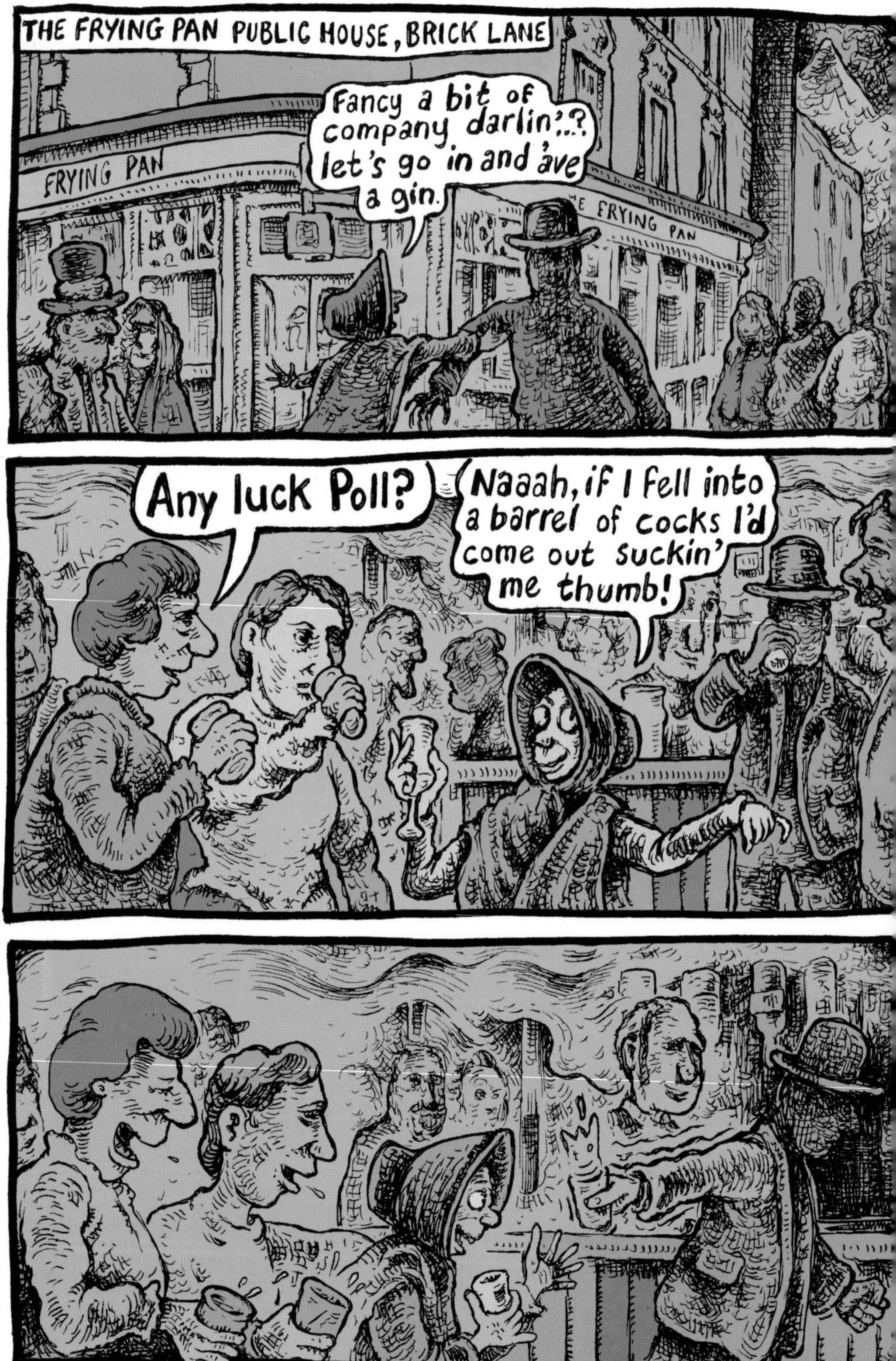
THE FRYING PAN PUBLIC HOUSE, BRICK LANE
FRYING PAN
Fancy a bit of company darlin'..? let's go in and 'ave a gin.
E FRYING PAN
Any luck Poll?
Naaah, if I fell into a barrel of cocks I'd come out suckin' me thumb!

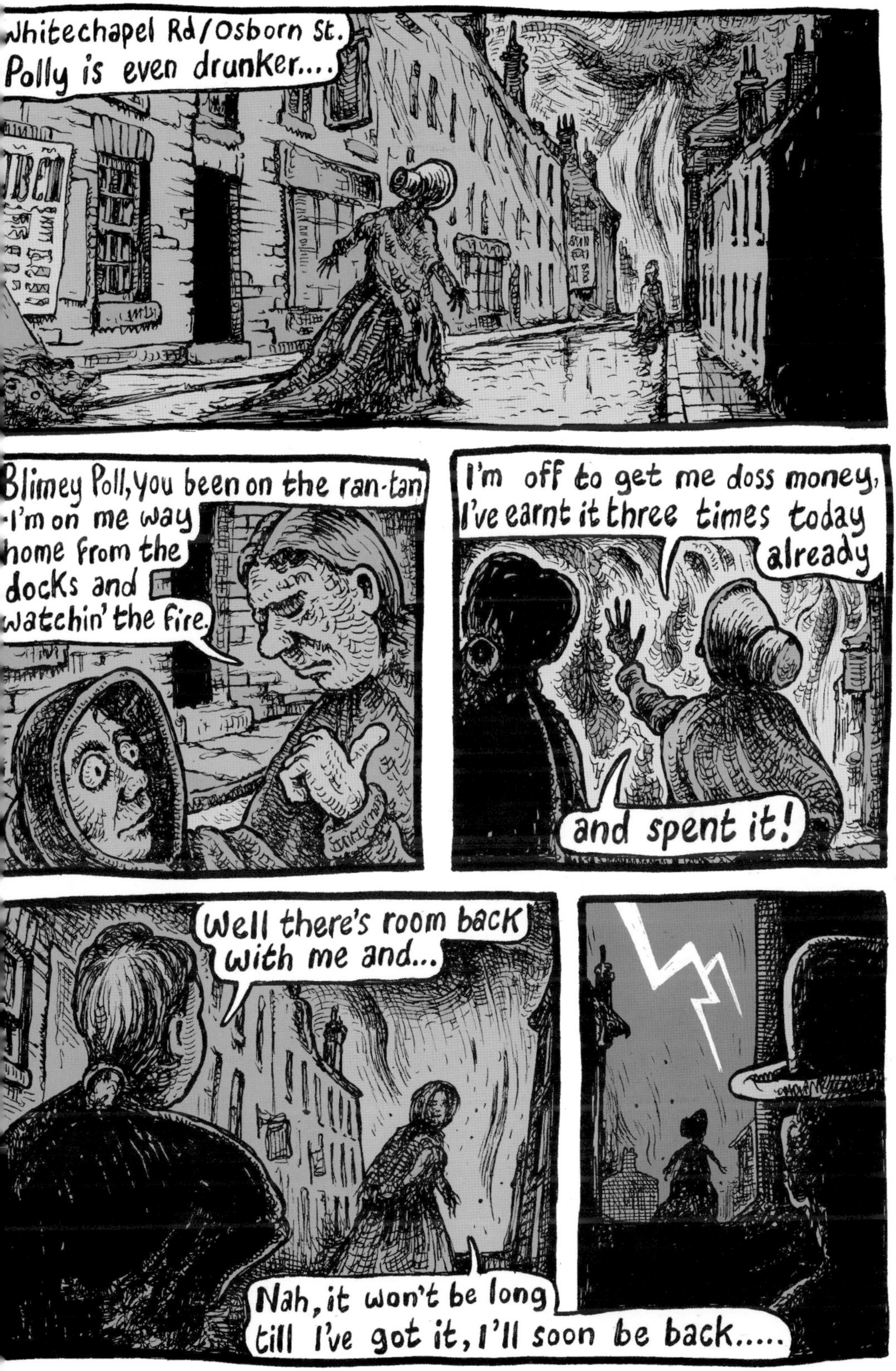
Whitechapel Rd/Osborn St.
Polly is even drunker....
Blimey Poll, you been on the ran-tan
-I'm on me way home from the docks and watchin' the fire.
I'm off to get me doss money, I've earnt it three times today already
and spent it!
Well there's room back with me and...
Nah, it won't be long till I've got it, I'll soon be back.....

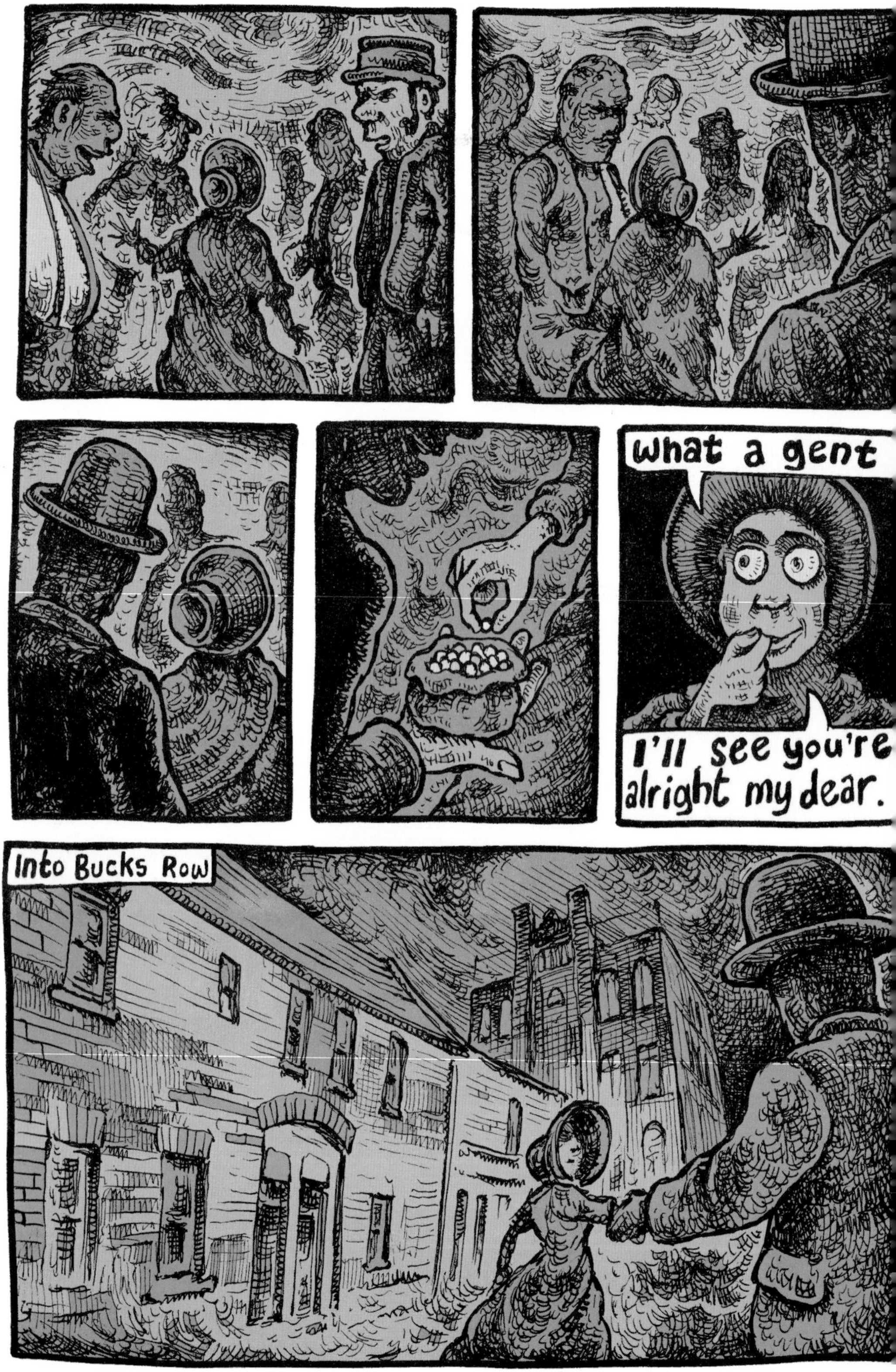
what a gent
I'll see you're alright my dear.
Into Bucks Row

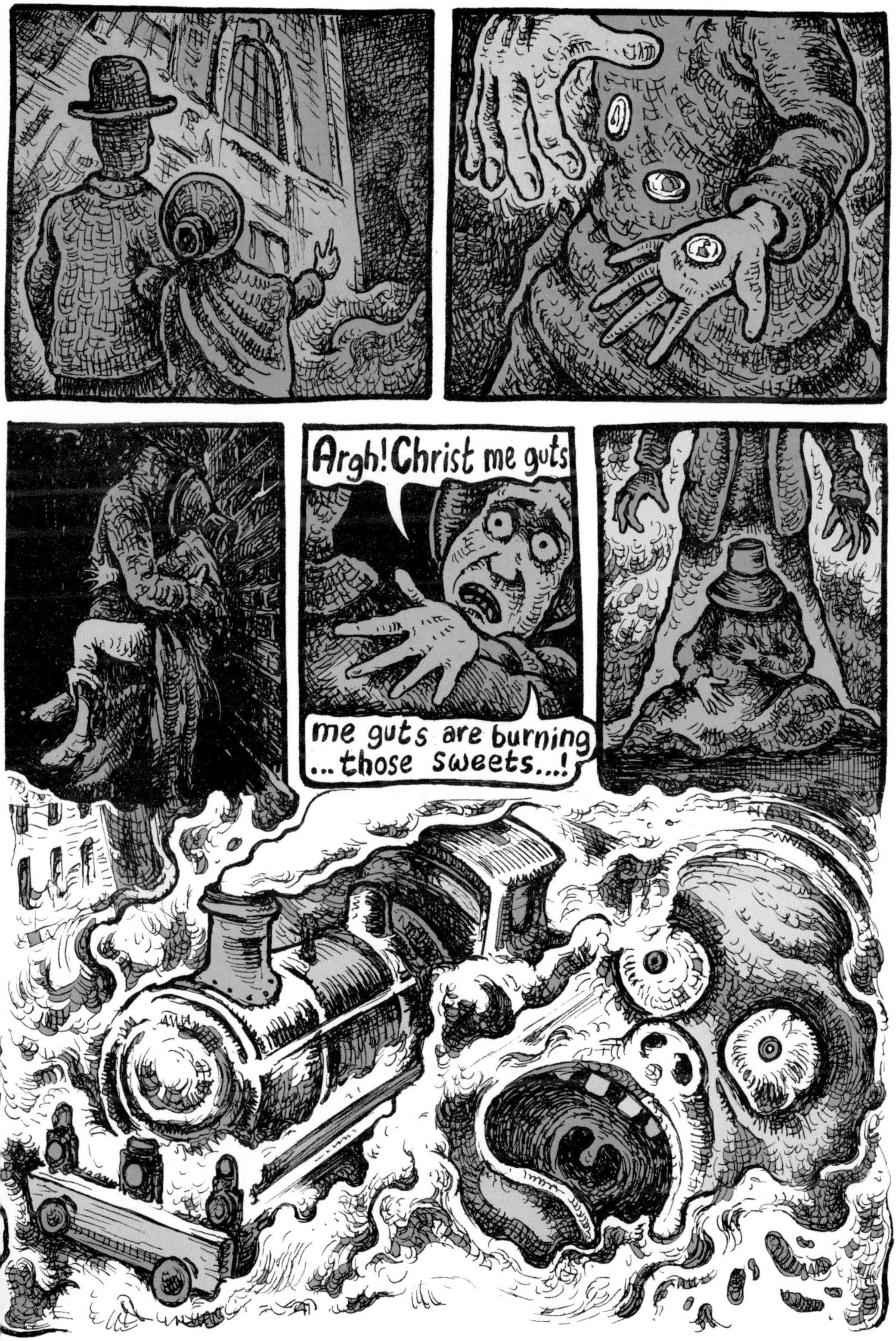
Argh! Christ me guts
me guts are burning
...those sweets...!

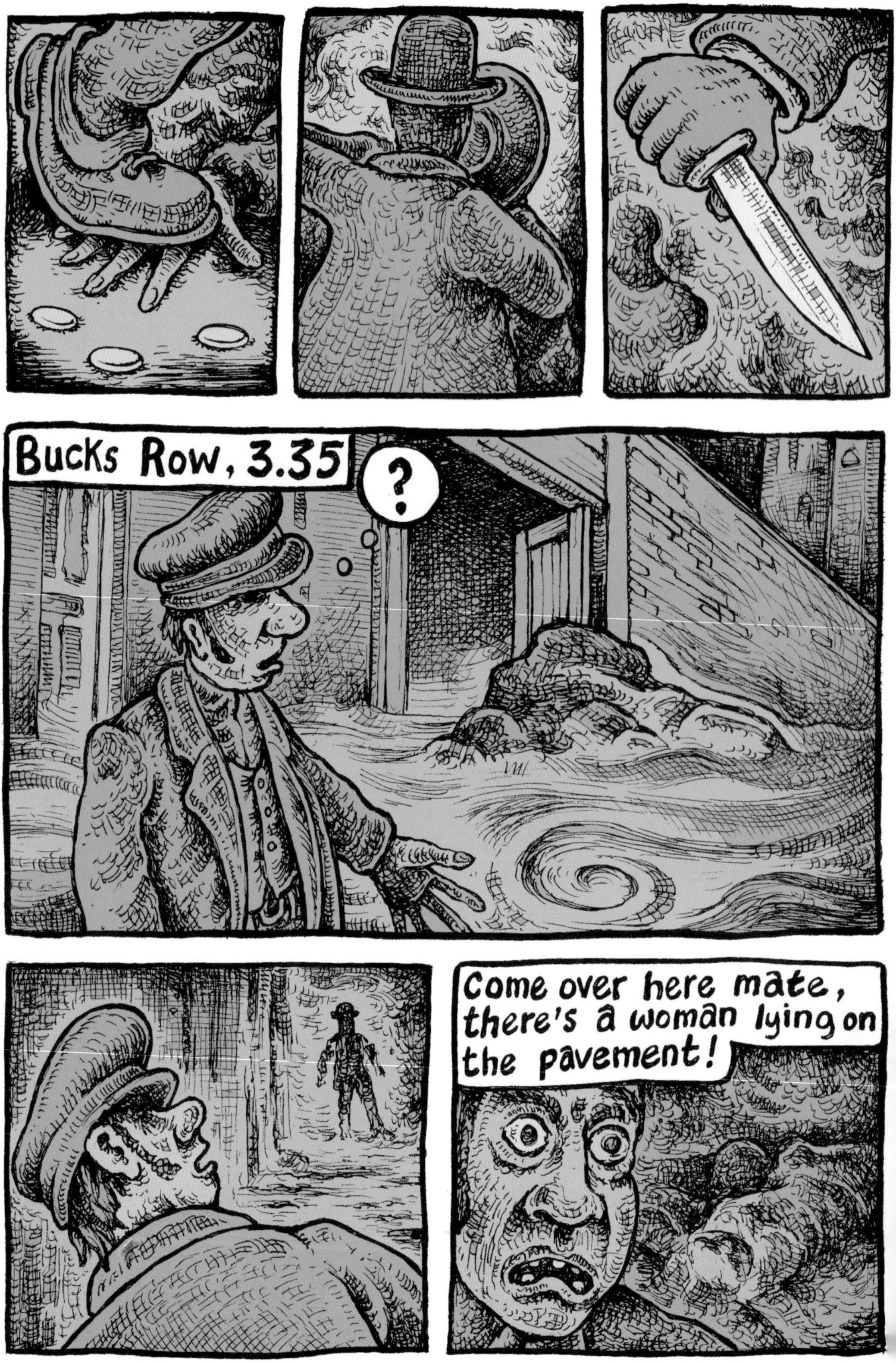
Bucks Row, 3.35
?
Come over here mate, there's a woman lying on the pavement!

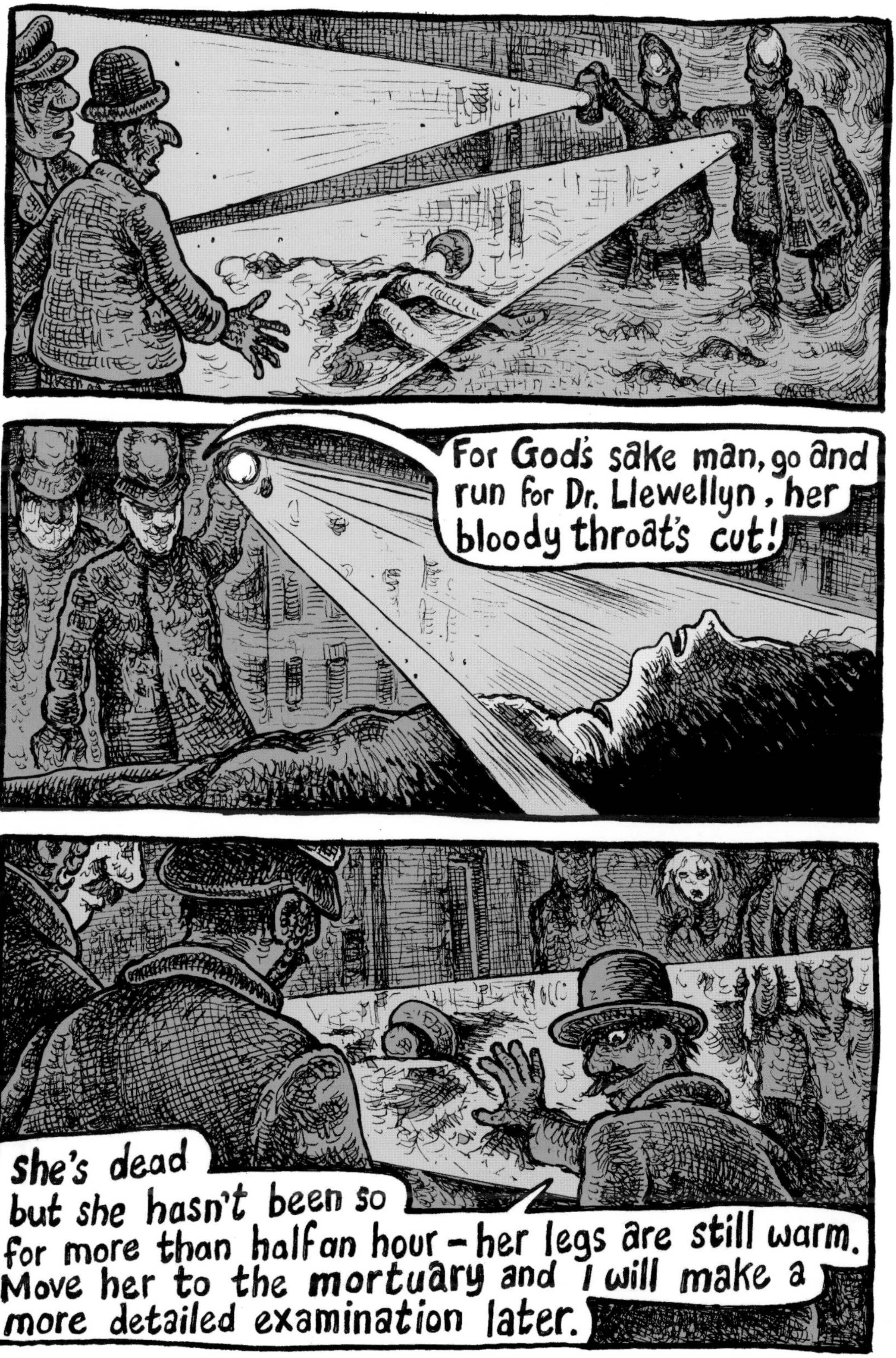
For God's sake man, go and run for Dr. Llewellyn, her bloody throat's cut!
she's dead
but she hasn't been so
for more than half an hour - her legs are still warm.
Move her to the mortuary and I will make a
more detailed examination later.

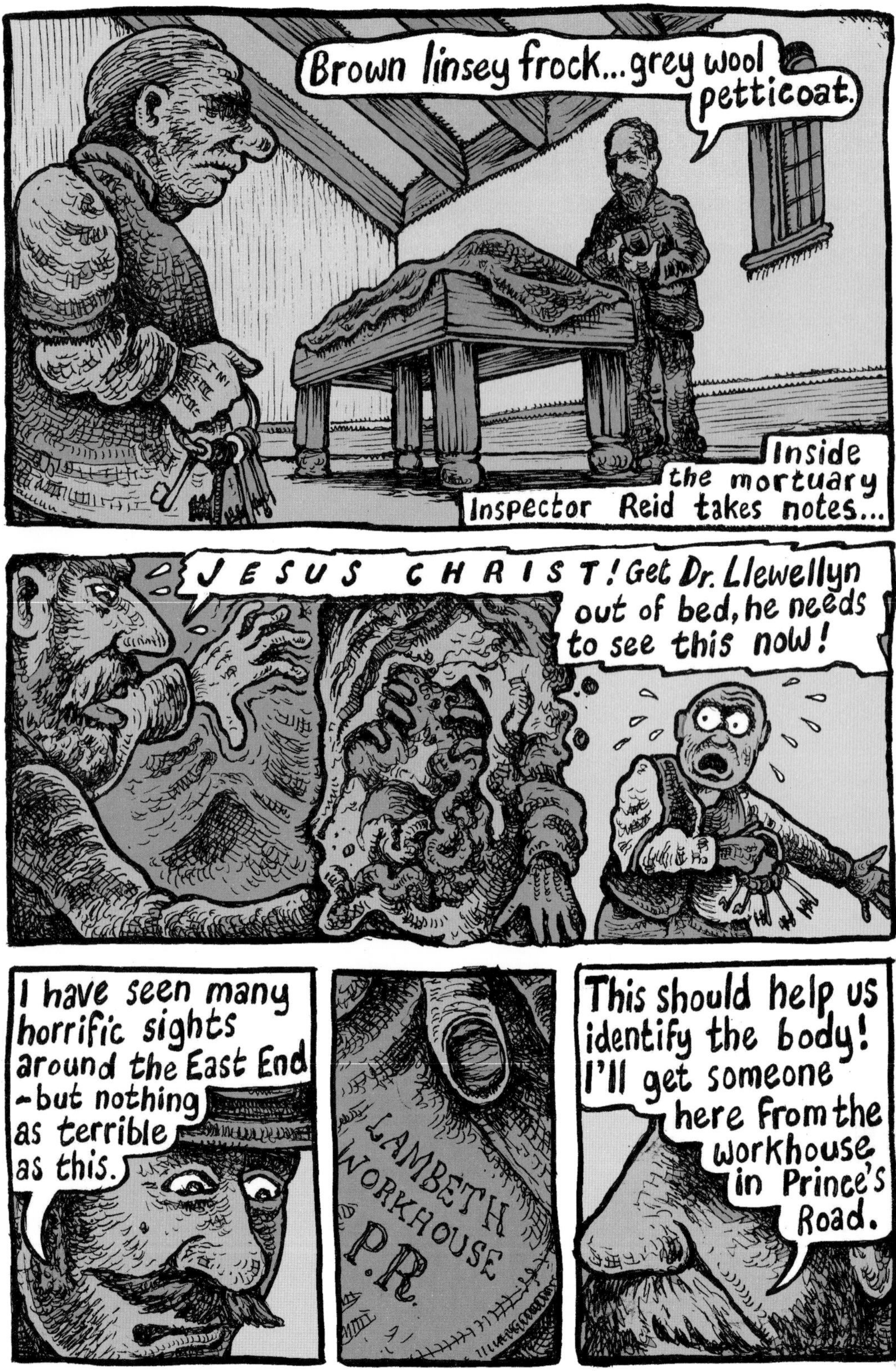
Brown linsey frock... grey wool petticoat.
Inside the mortuary Inspector Reid takes notes...
JESUS CHRIST! Get Dr. Llewellyn out of bed, he needs to see this now!
I have seen many horrific sights around the East End - but nothing as terrible as this.
LAMBETH WORKHOUSE P.R.
This should help us identify the body! I'll get someone here from the workhouse in Prince's Road.

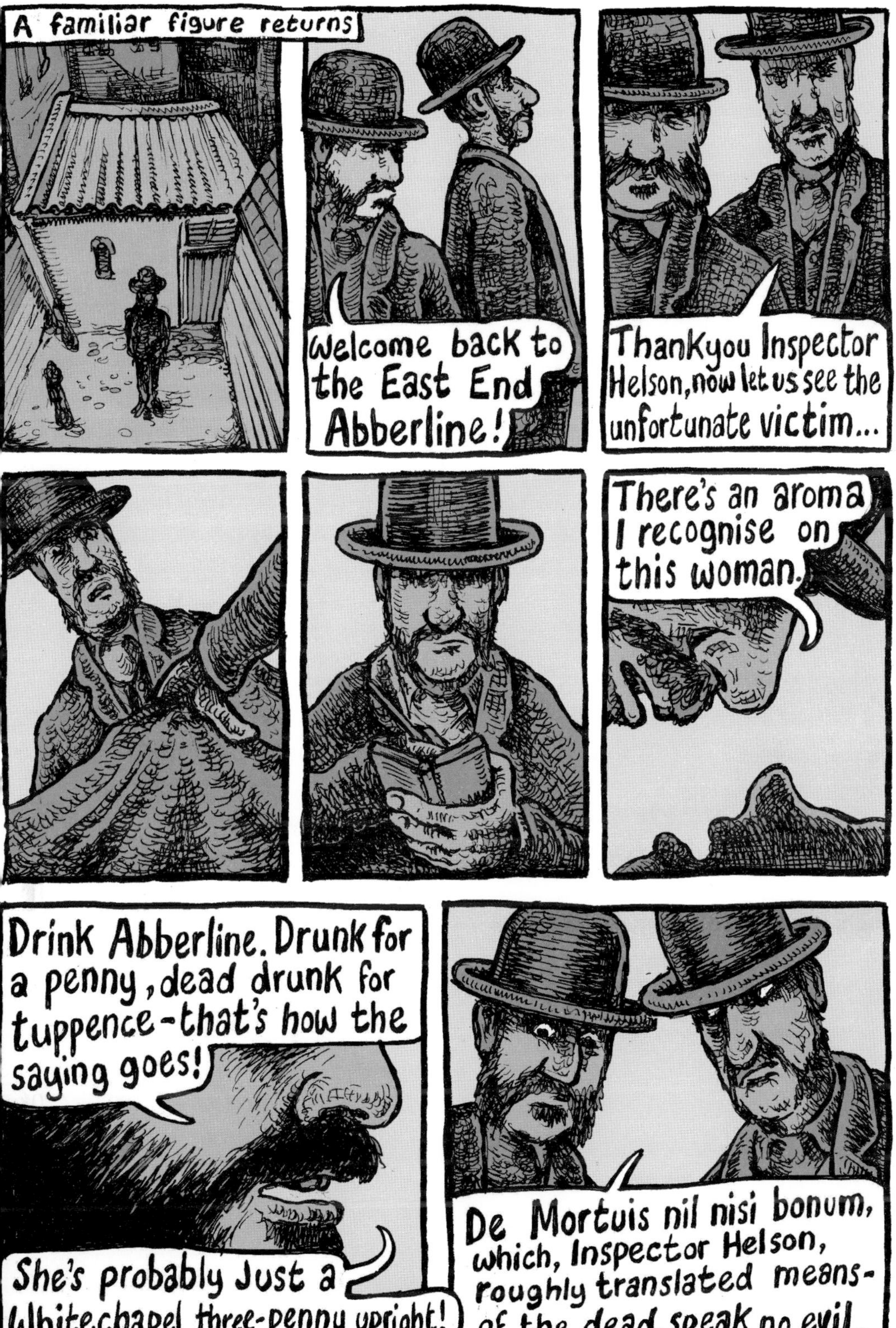
A familiar figure returns
Welcome back to the East End Abberline!
Thankyou Inspector Helson, now let us see the unfortunate victim...
There's an aroma I recognise on this woman.
Drink Abberline. Drunk for a penny, dead drunk for tuppence - that's how the saying goes!
She's probably Just a Whitechapel three-penny upright!
De Mortuis nil nisi bonum, which, Inspector Helson, roughly translated means - of the dead, speak no evil.

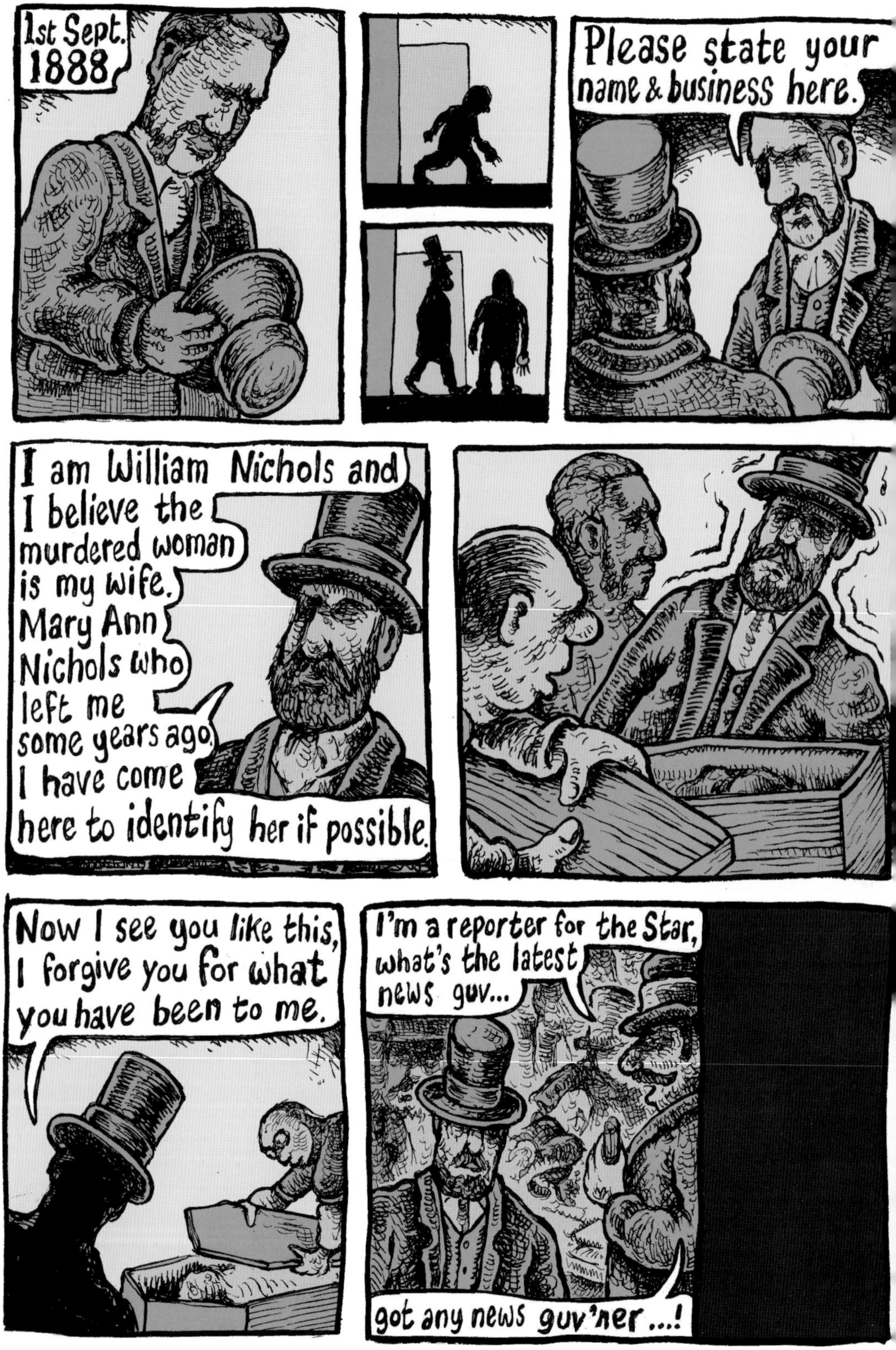
1st Sept. 1888
Please state your name & business here.
I am William Nichols and I believe the murdered woman is my wife. Mary Ann Nichols who left me some years ago. I have come here to identify her if possible.
Now I see you like this, I forgive you for what you have been to me.
I'm a reporter for the Star, what's the latest news guv...
got any news guv'ner ...!

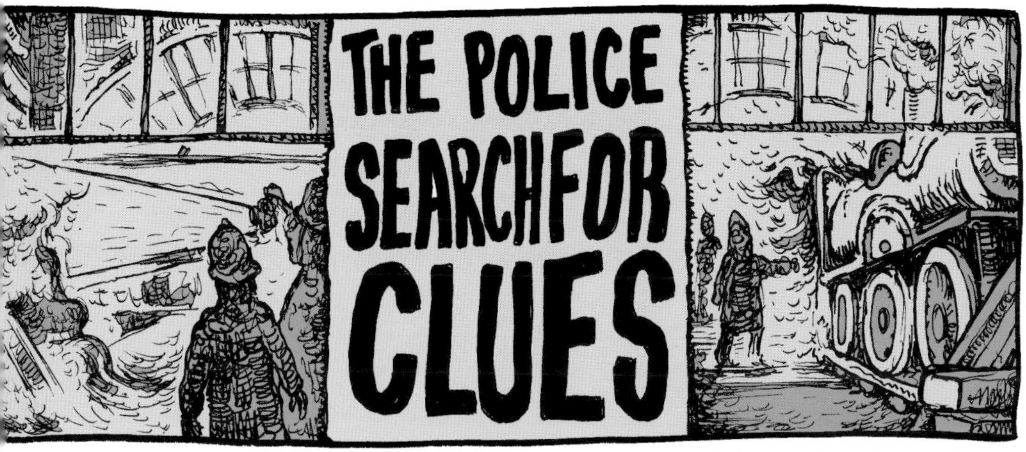
THE POLICE SEARCH FOR CLUES

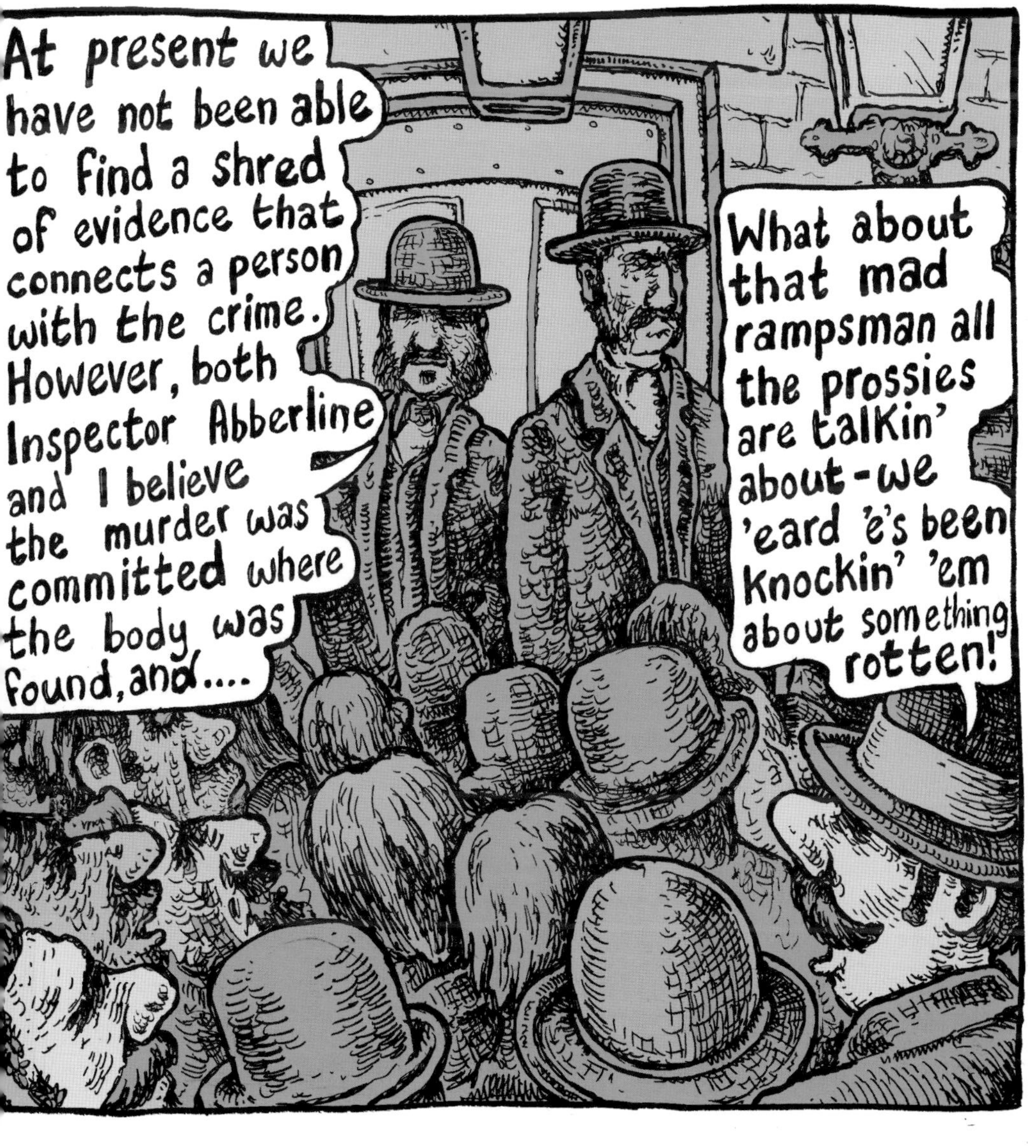
At present we have not been able to find a shred of evidence that connects a person with the crime. However, both Inspector Abberline and I believe the murder was committed where the body was found, and....
What about that mad rampsman all the prossies are talkin' about - we 'eard 'e's been knockin' 'em about something rotten!

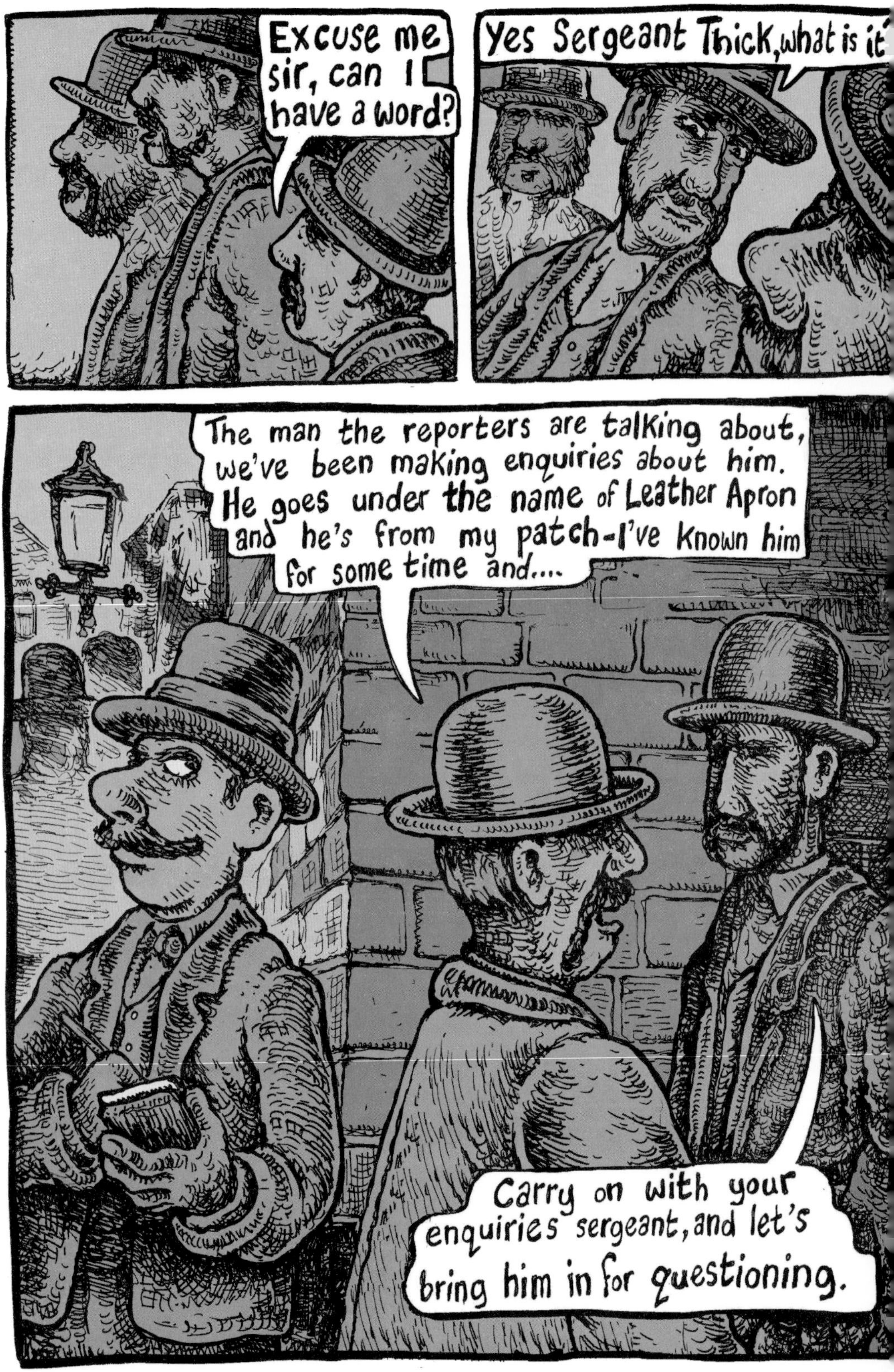
Excuse me sir, can I have a word?
Yes Sergeant Thick, what is it?
The man the reporters are talking about, we've been making enquiries about him. He goes under the name of Leather Apron and he's from my patch-I've known him for some time and....
Carry on with your enquiries sergeant, and let's bring him in for questioning.

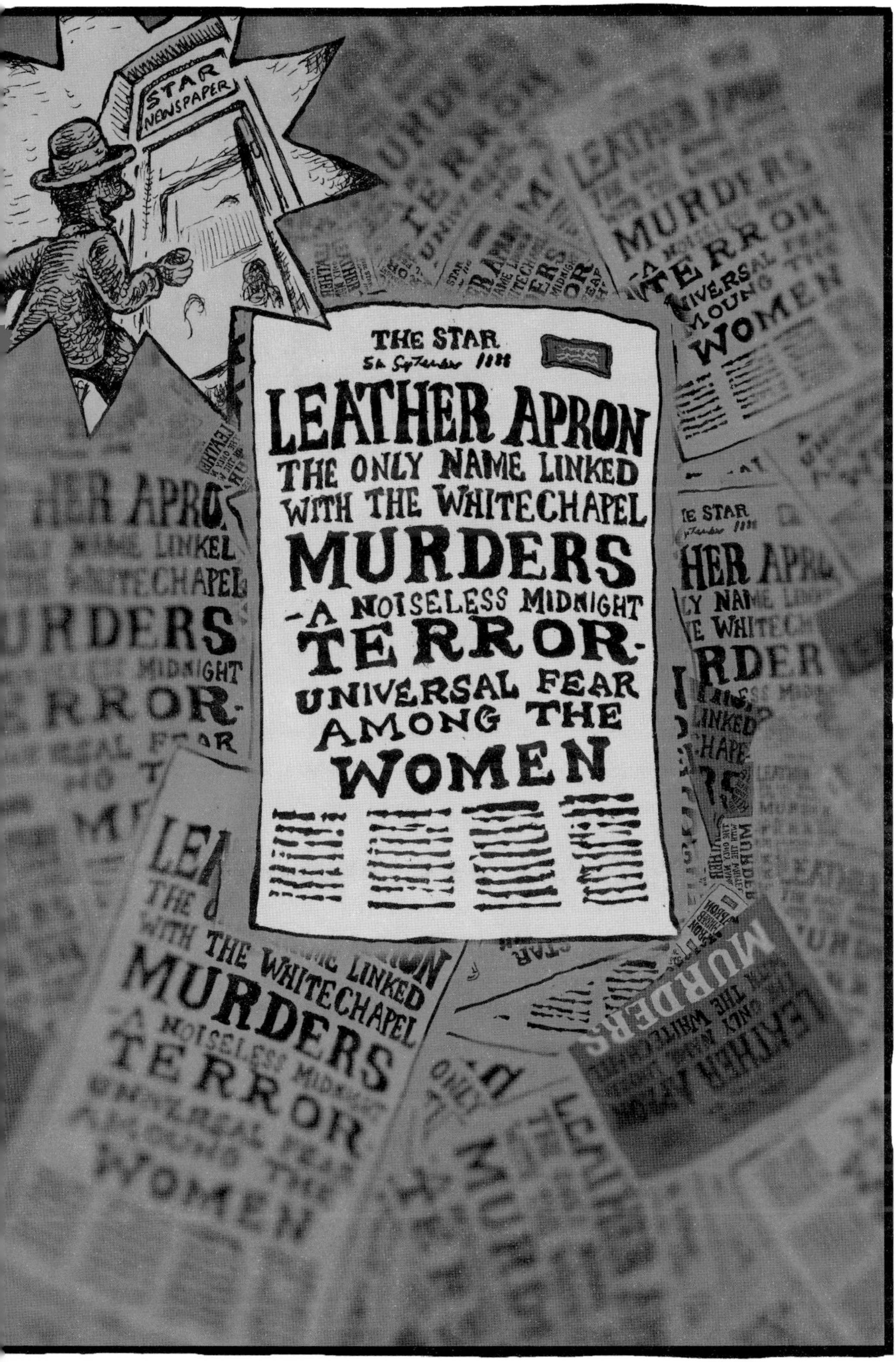

STAR NEWSPAPER
THE STAR
LEATHER APRON
THE ONLY NAME LINKED
WITH THE WHITECHAPEL
MURDERS
-A NOISELESS MIDNIGHT
TERROR-
UNIVERSAL FEAR
AMONG THE
WOMEN

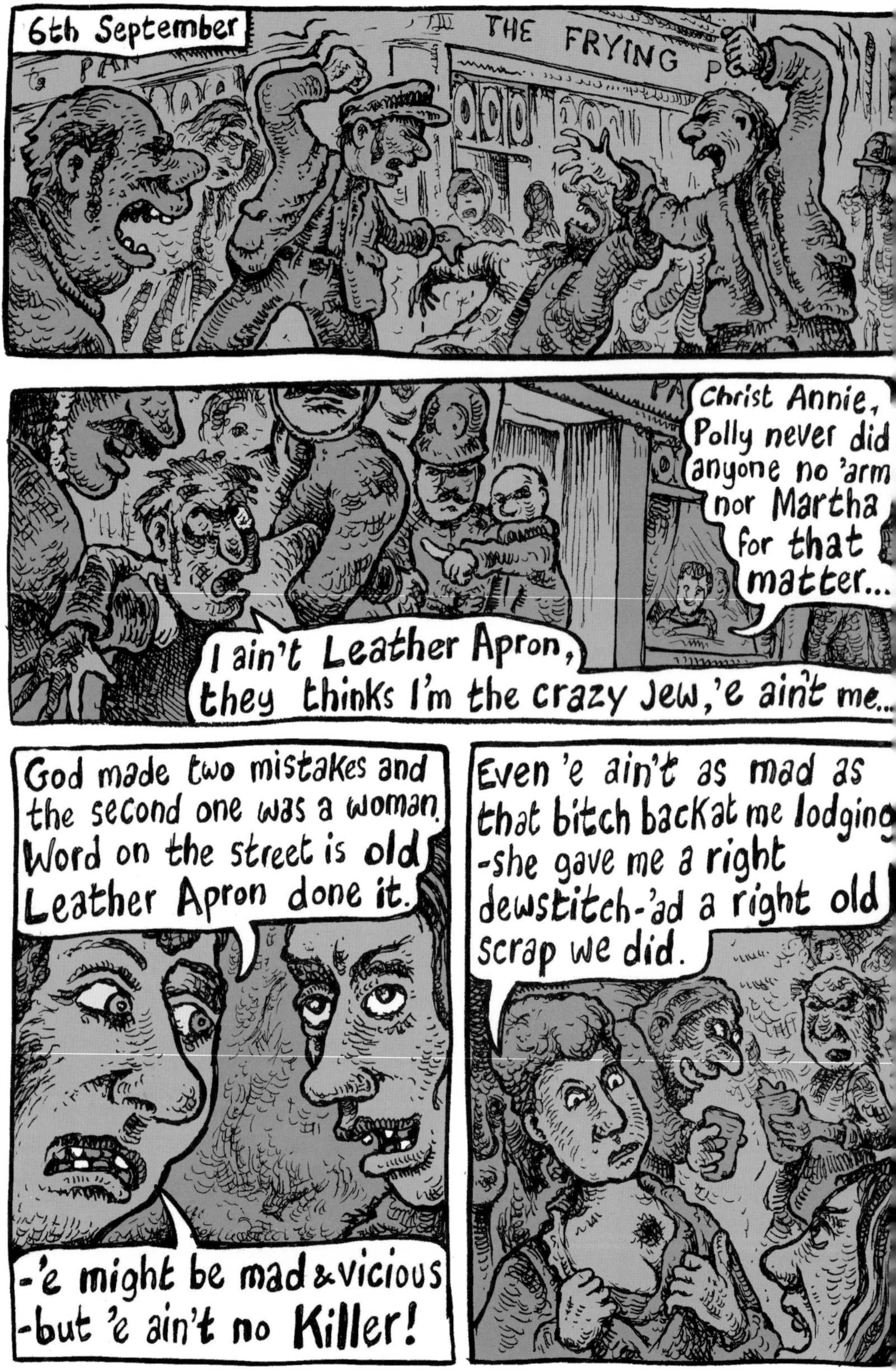
6th September
THE FRYING P
Christ Annie, Polly never did anyone no 'arm nor Martha for that matter...
I ain't Leather Apron, they thinks I'm the crazy Jew, 'e ain't me...
God made two mistakes and the second one was a woman. Word on the street is old Leather Apron done it.
-'e might be mad & vicious -but 'e ain't no Killer!
Even 'e ain't as mad as that bitch back at me lodging -she gave me a right dewstitch-'ad a right old scrap we did.

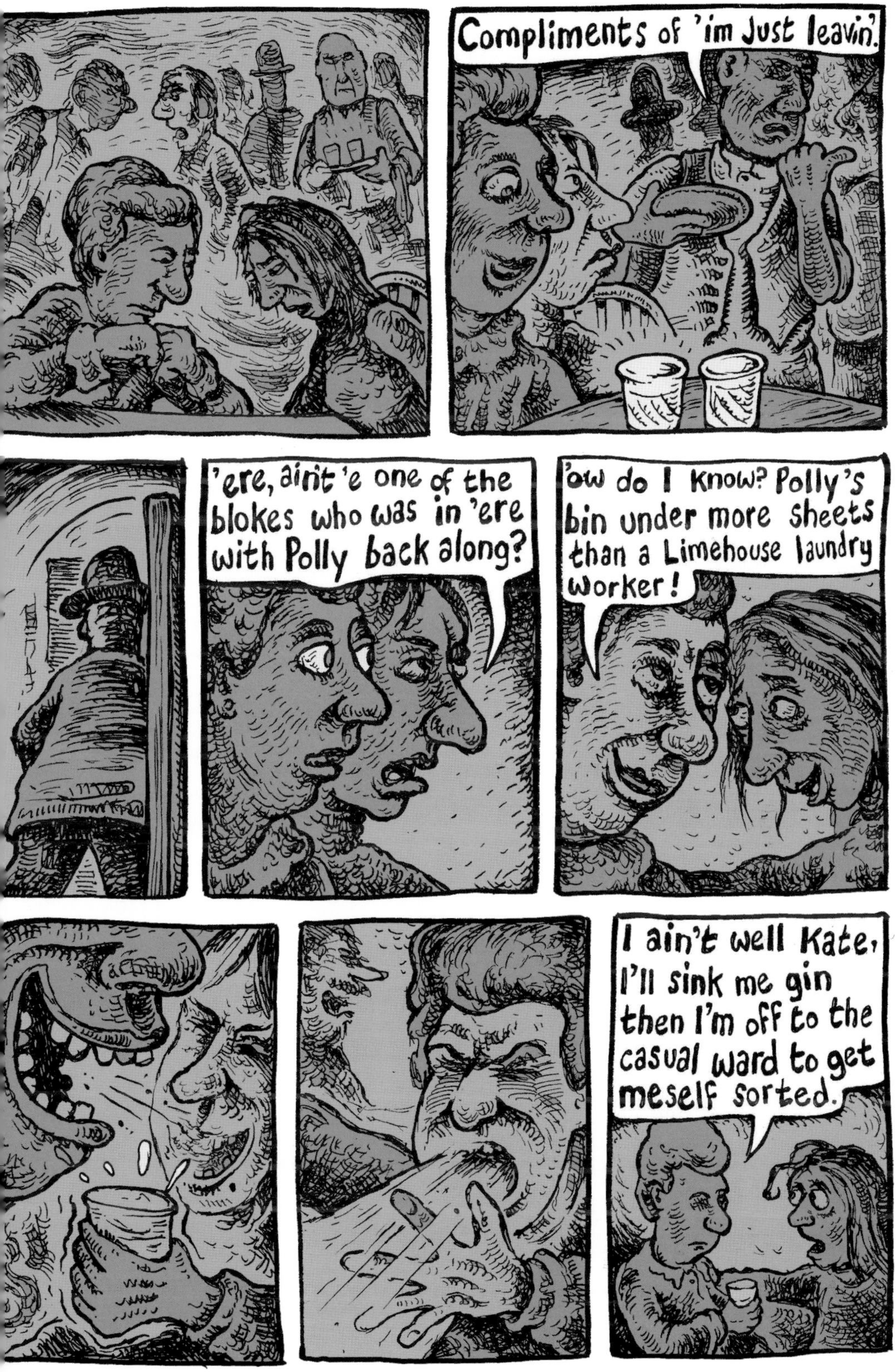
Compliments of 'im just leavin'.
'ere, ain't 'e one of the blokes who was in 'ere with Polly back along?
'ow do I know? Polly's bin under more sheets than a Limehouse laundry worker!
I ain't well Kate, I'll sink me gin then I'm off to the casual ward to get meself sorted.

The next day, 5:00pm - Annie Chapman stands in Dorset street

You still 'ere Annie?

I'm 'ere to get some money for me lodgings but I don't know 'ow, I'm ill and feels proper rotten

1·30am
CROSSINGHAM'S LODGING HOUSE

Mr. Donovan says you know the rules Annie: no money-no bed!

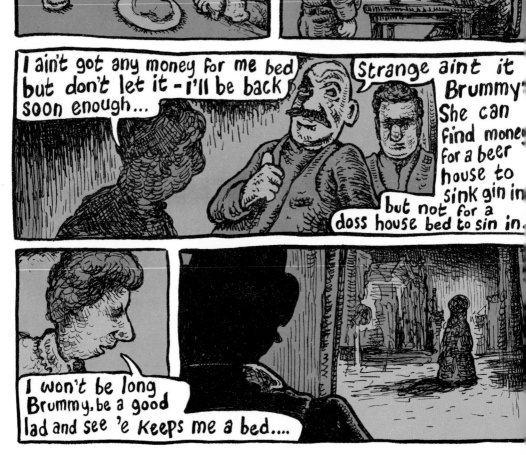

I ain't got any money for me bed but don't let it - i'll be back soon enough...

Strange aint it Brummy? She can find money for a beer house to sink gin in but not for a doss house bed to sin in.

I won't be long Brummy, be a good lad and see 'e keeps me a bed....

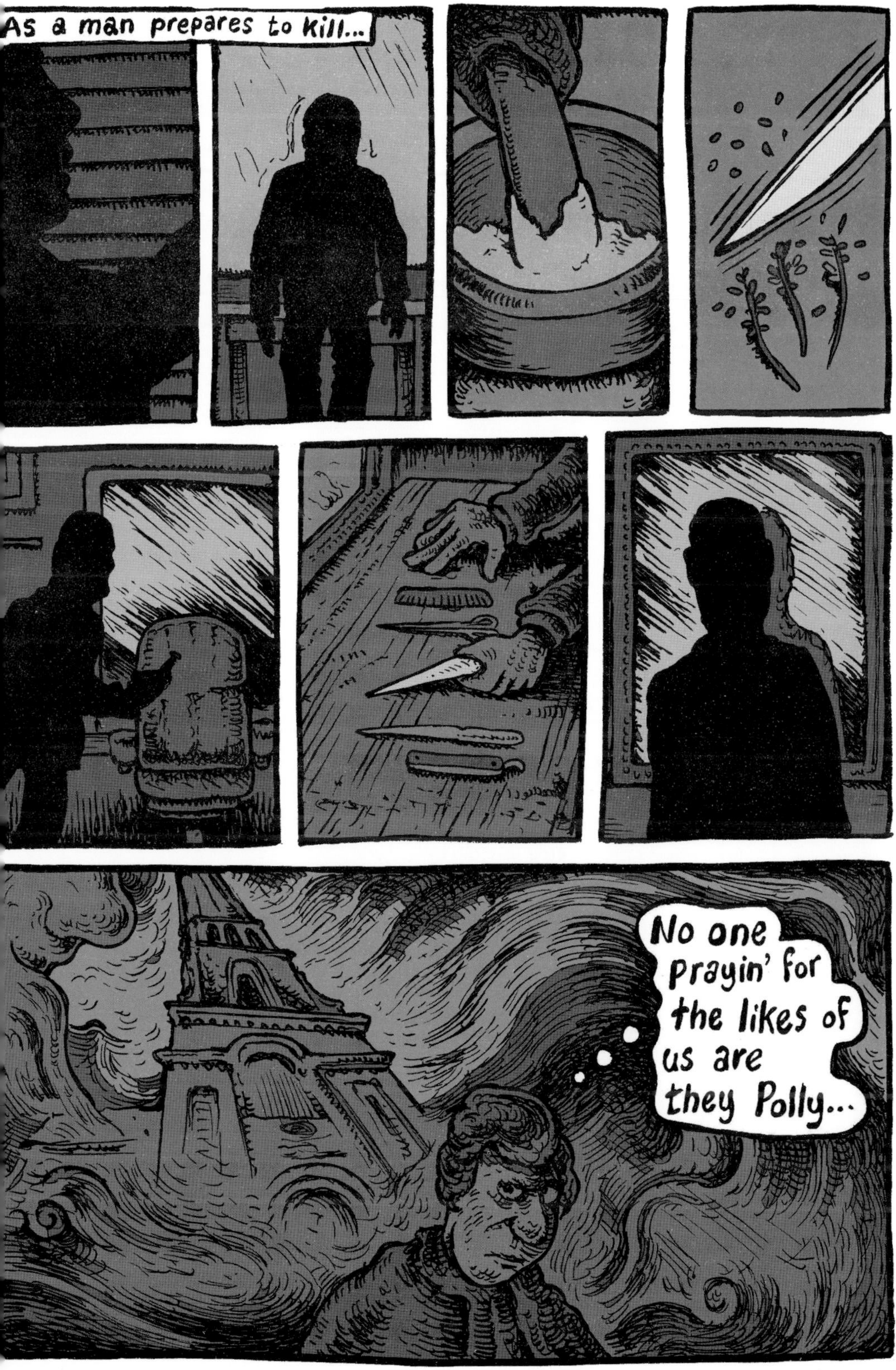
As a man prepares to kill...
No one prayin' for the likes of us are they Polly...

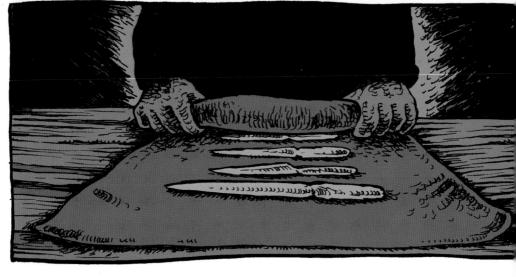

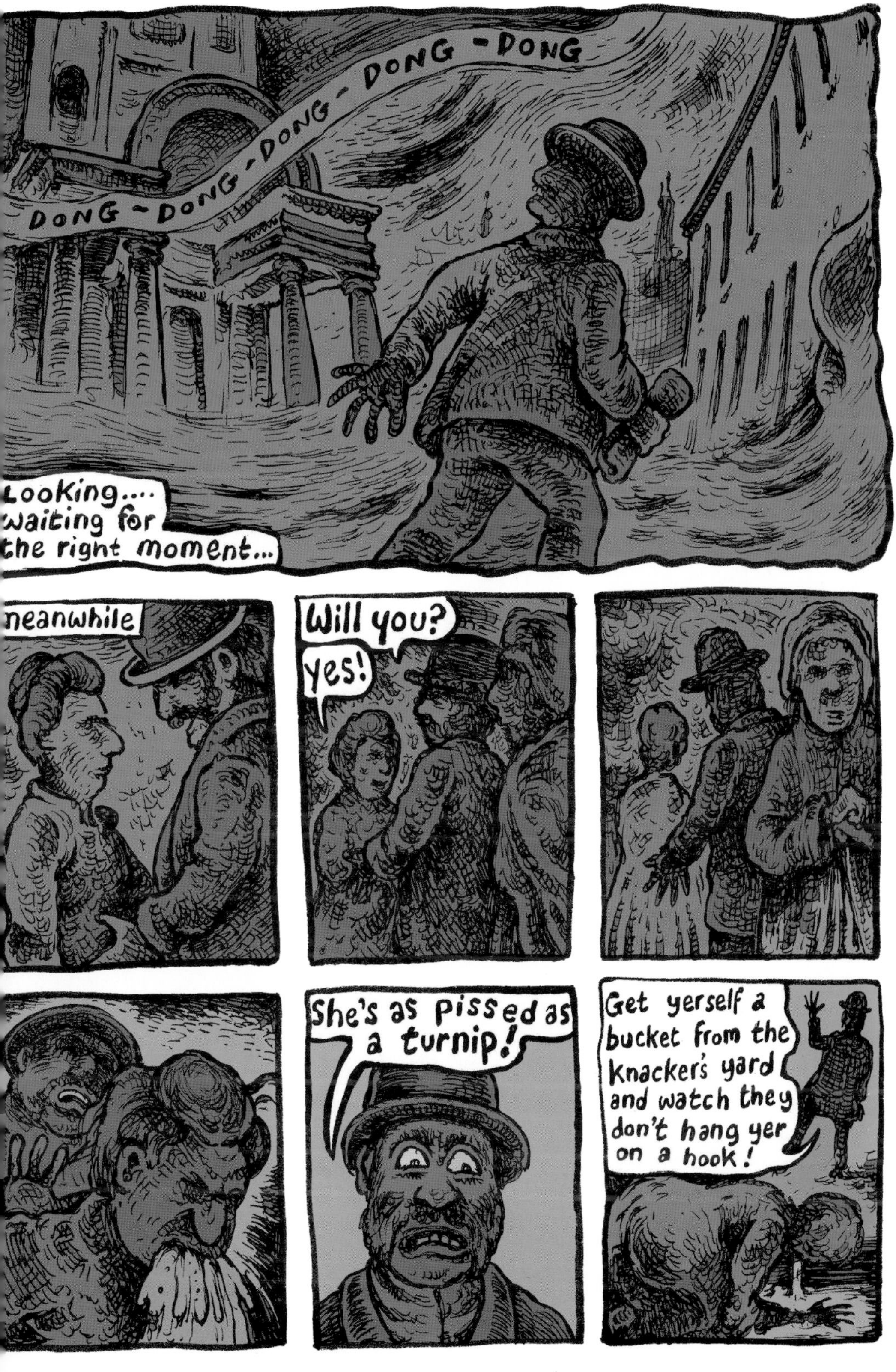
DONG - DONG - DONG - DONG - DONG
Looking.... waiting for the right moment...
meanwhile
Will you?
Yes!
She's as pissed as a turnip!
Get yerself a bucket from the knacker's yard and watch they don't hang yer on a hook!

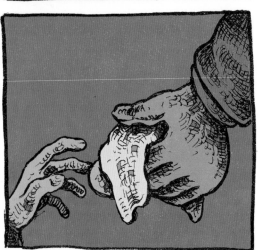

Tar old cock, come with me down 'ere.

NO!

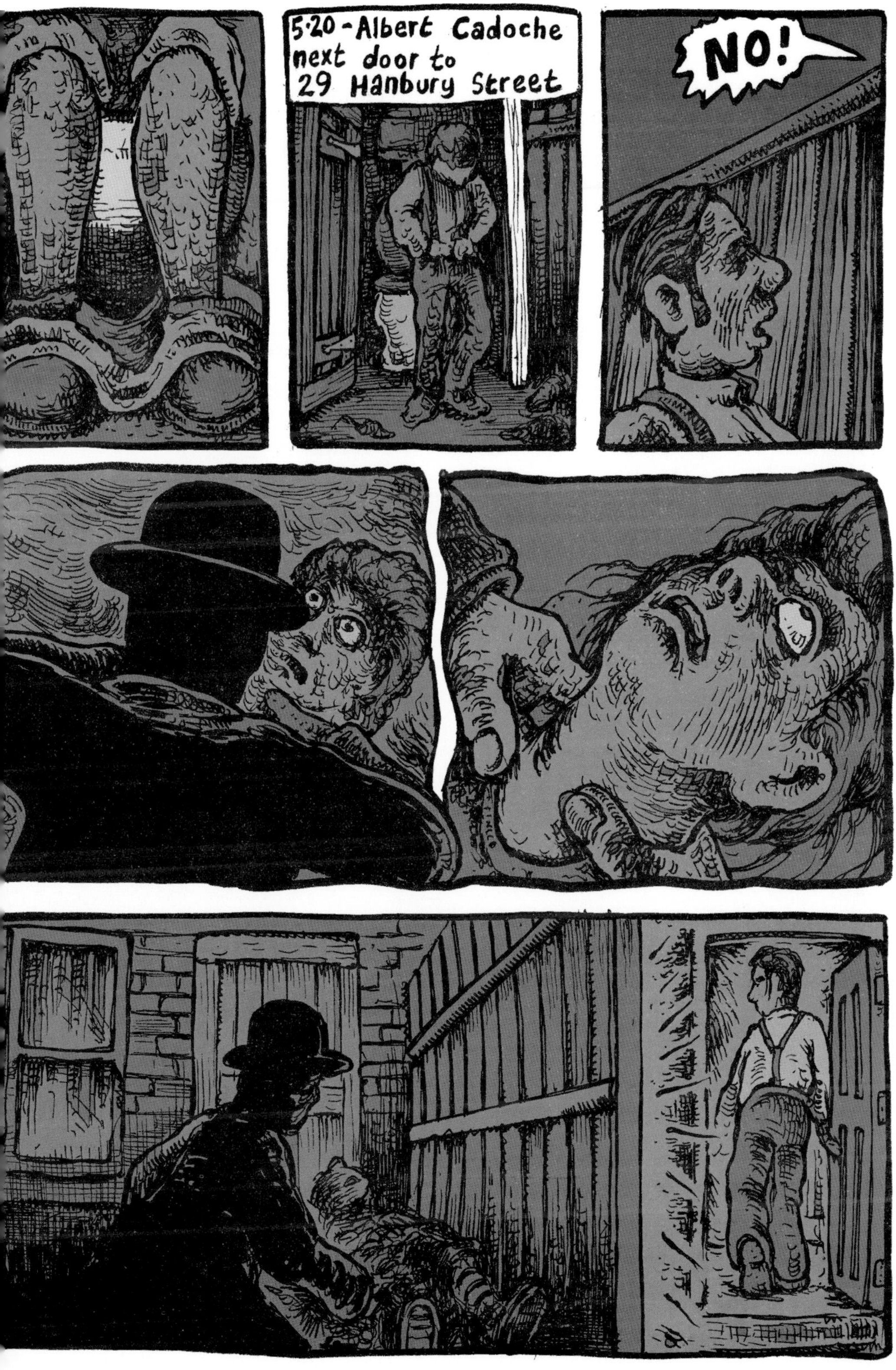
5·20 - Albert Cadoche
next door to
29 Hanbury Street
NO!

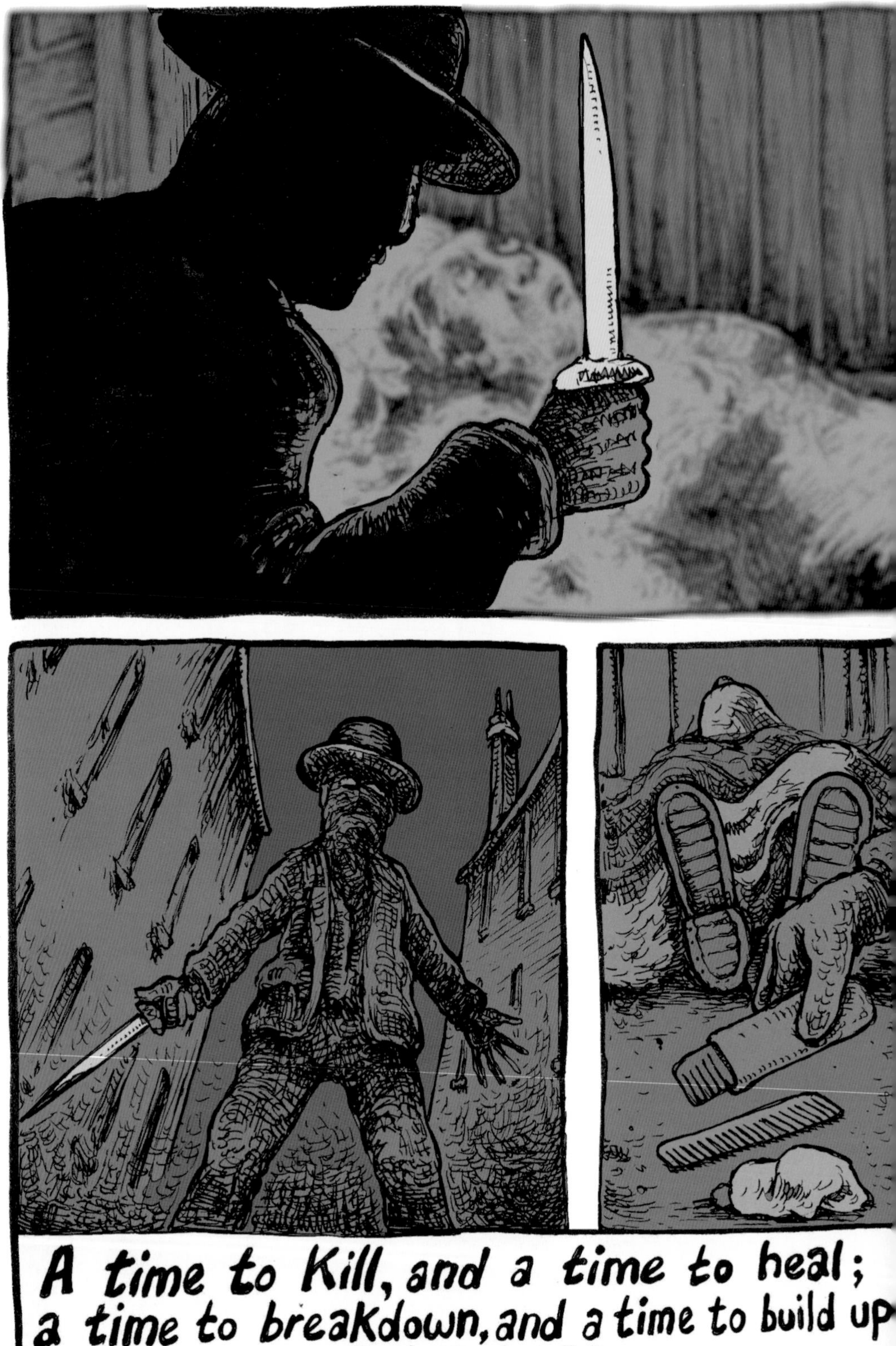
A time to Kill, and a time to heal;
a time to breakdown, and a time to build up
Ecclesiastes 3:3

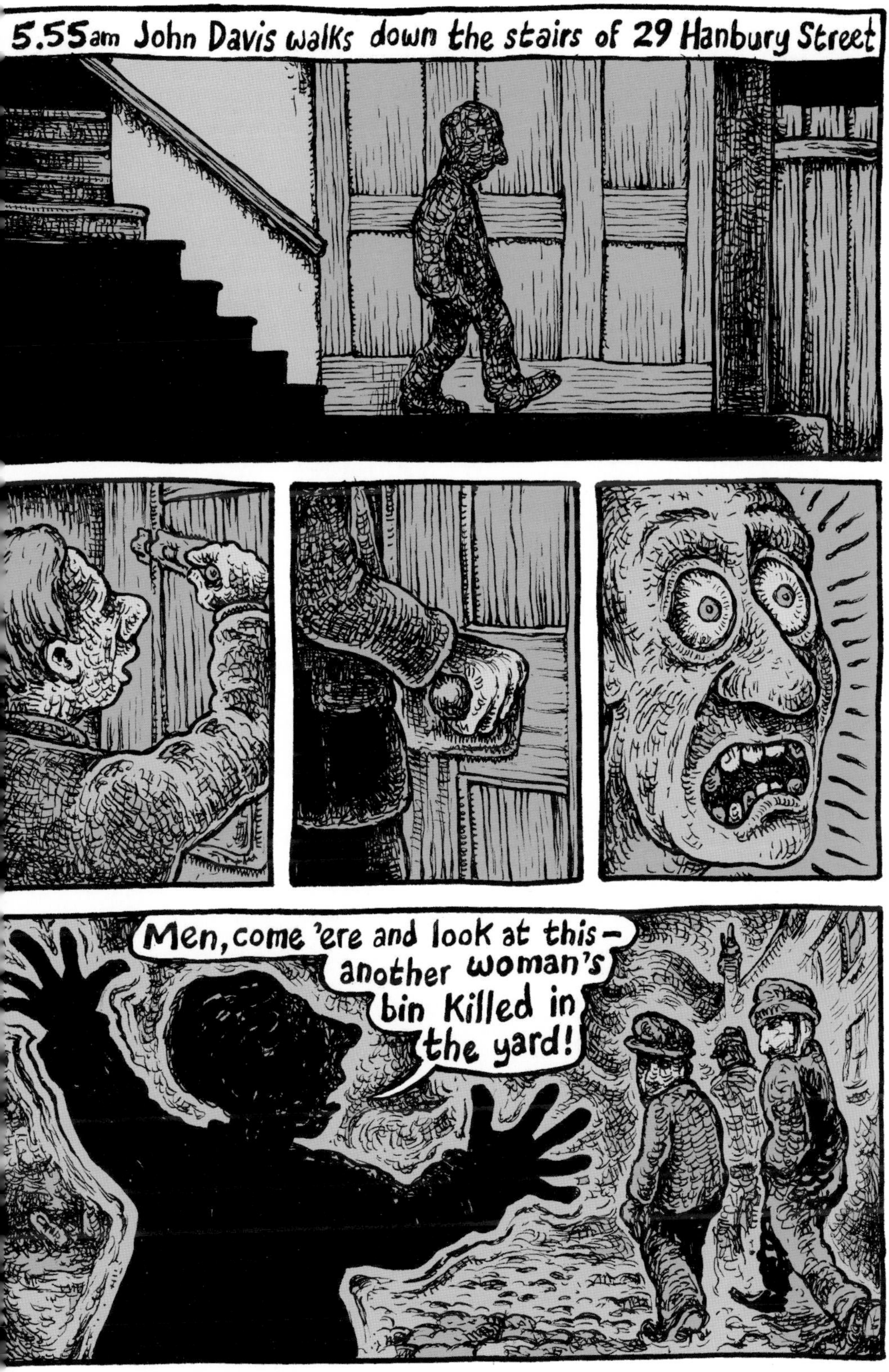
5.55am John Davis walks down the stairs of 29 Hanbury Street
Men, come 'ere and look at this – another woman's bin Killed in the yard!

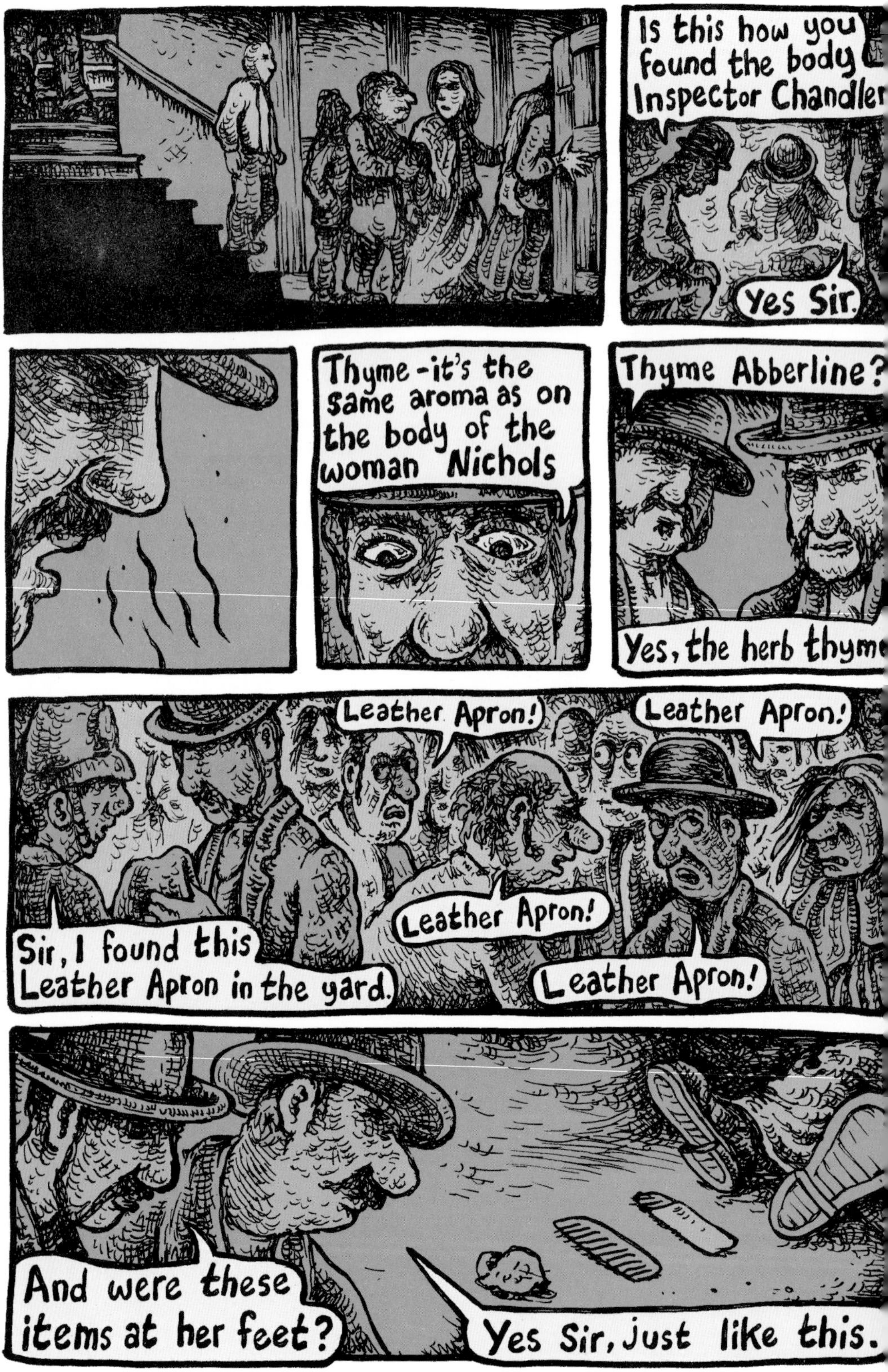
Is this how you found the body Inspector Chandler
Yes Sir.
Thyme - it's the same aroma as on the body of the woman Nichols
Thyme Abberline?
Yes, the herb thyme
Leather Apron!
Leather Apron!
Sir, I found this Leather Apron in the yard.
Leather Apron!
Leather Apron!
And were these items at her feet?
Yes Sir, just like this.

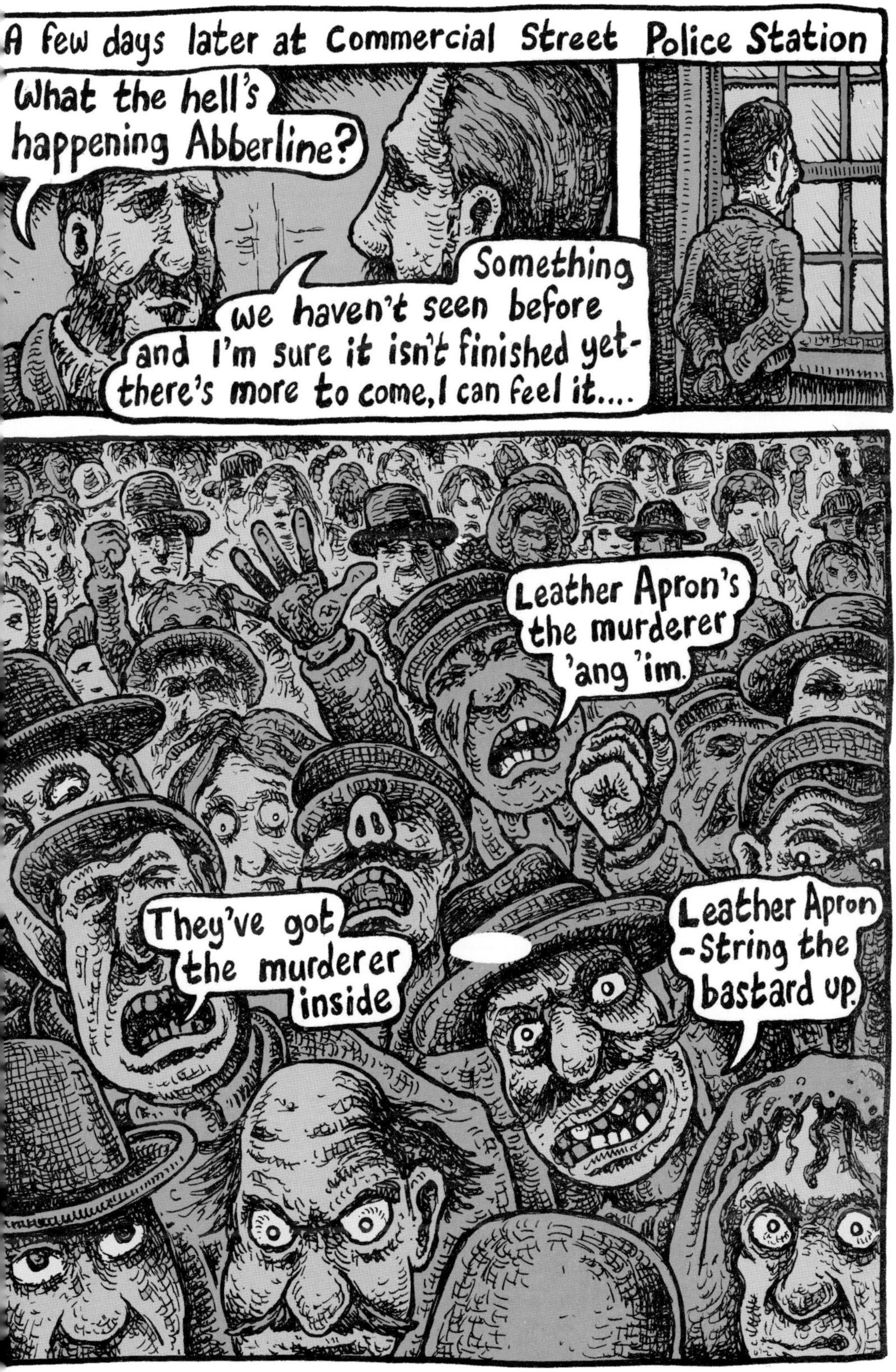
A few days later at Commercial Street Police Station
What the hell's happening Abberline?
Something we haven't seen before and I'm sure it isn't finished yet- there's more to come, I can feel it....
Leather Apron's the murderer 'ang 'im.
They've got the murderer inside
Leather Apron -String the bastard up.

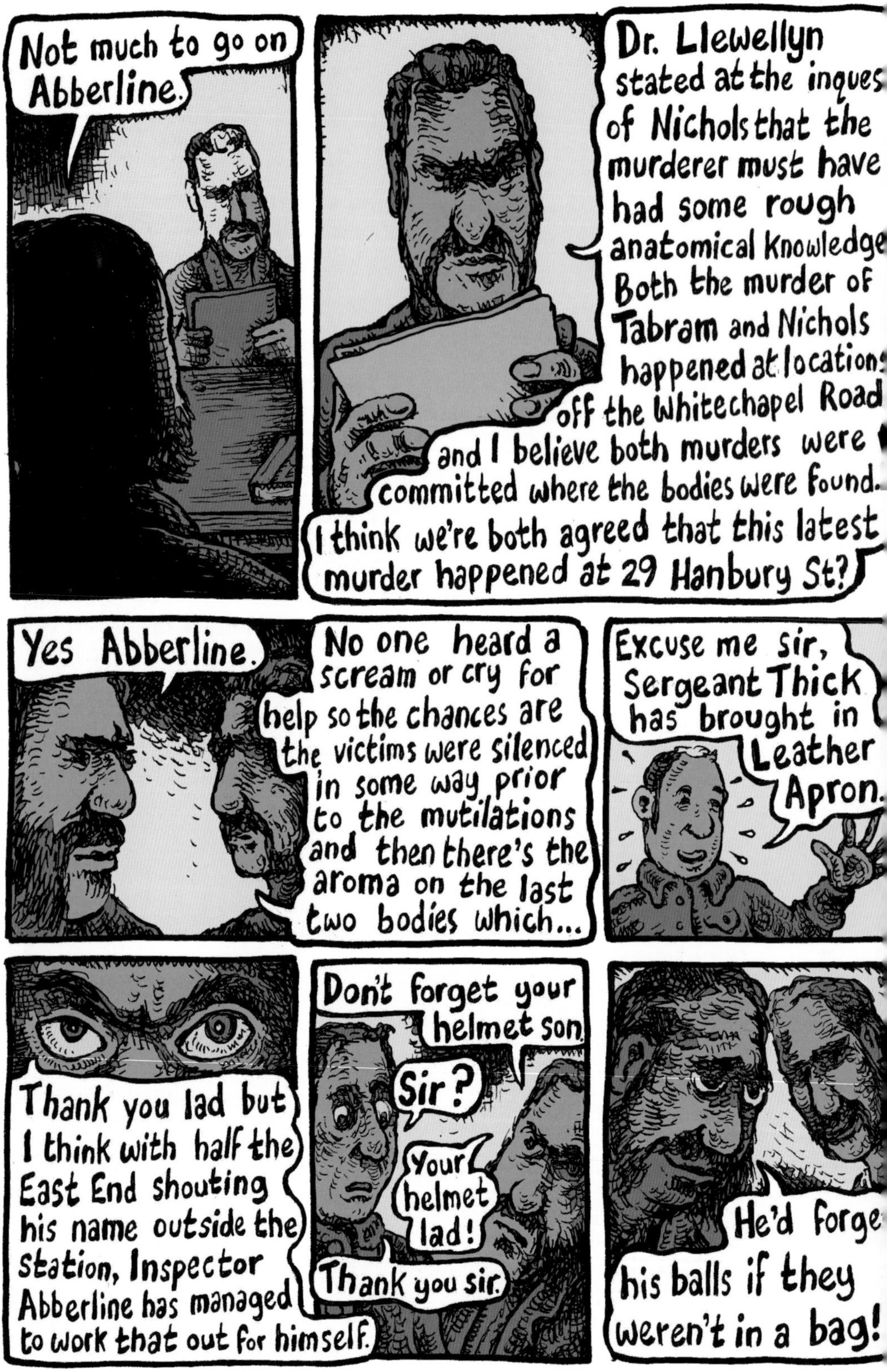
Not much to go on Abberline.
Dr. Llewellyn stated at the inques of Nichols that the murderer must have had some rough anatomical knowledge Both the murder of Tabram and Nichols happened at locations off the Whitechapel Road and I believe both murders were committed where the bodies were found.
I think we're both agreed that this latest murder happened at 29 Hanbury St?
Yes Abberline.
No one heard a scream or cry for help so the chances are the victims were silenced in some way prior to the mutilations and then there's the aroma on the last two bodies which...
Excuse me sir, Sergeant Thick has brought in Leather Apron.
Thank you lad but I think with half the East End shouting his name outside the station, Inspector Abberline has managed to work that out for himself.
Don't forget your helmet son.
Sir?
Your helmet lad!
Thank you sir.
He'd forge his balls if they weren't in a bag!

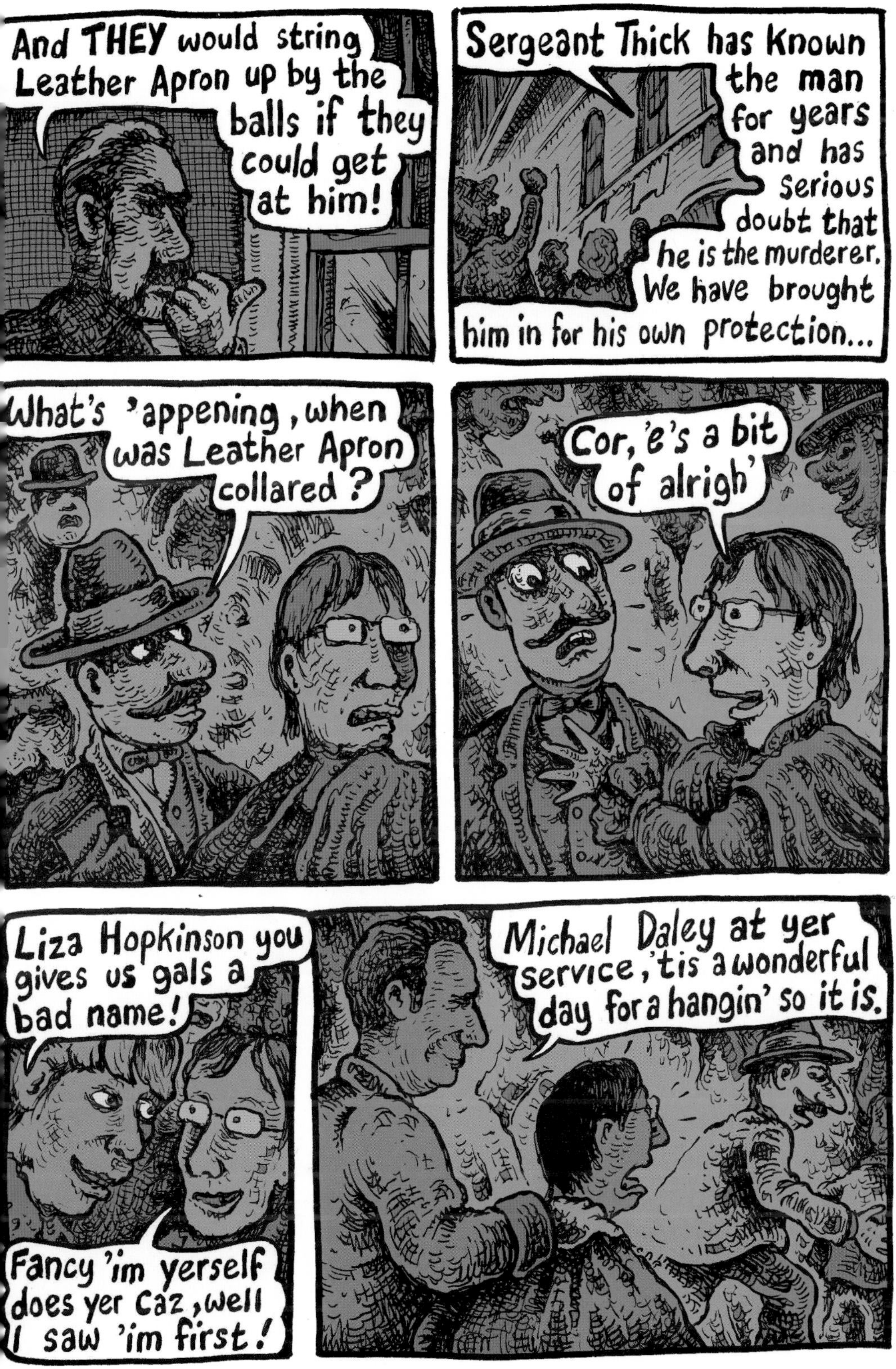
And THEY would string Leather Apron up by the balls if they could get at him!
Sergeant Thick has known the man for years and has serious doubt that he is the murderer. We have brought him in for his own protection...
What's 'appening, when was Leather Apron collared?
Cor, 'e's a bit of alrigh'
Liza Hopkinson you gives us gals a bad name!
Fancy 'im yerself does yer Caz, well I saw 'im first!
Michael Daley at yer service, 'tis a wonderful day for a hangin' so it is.

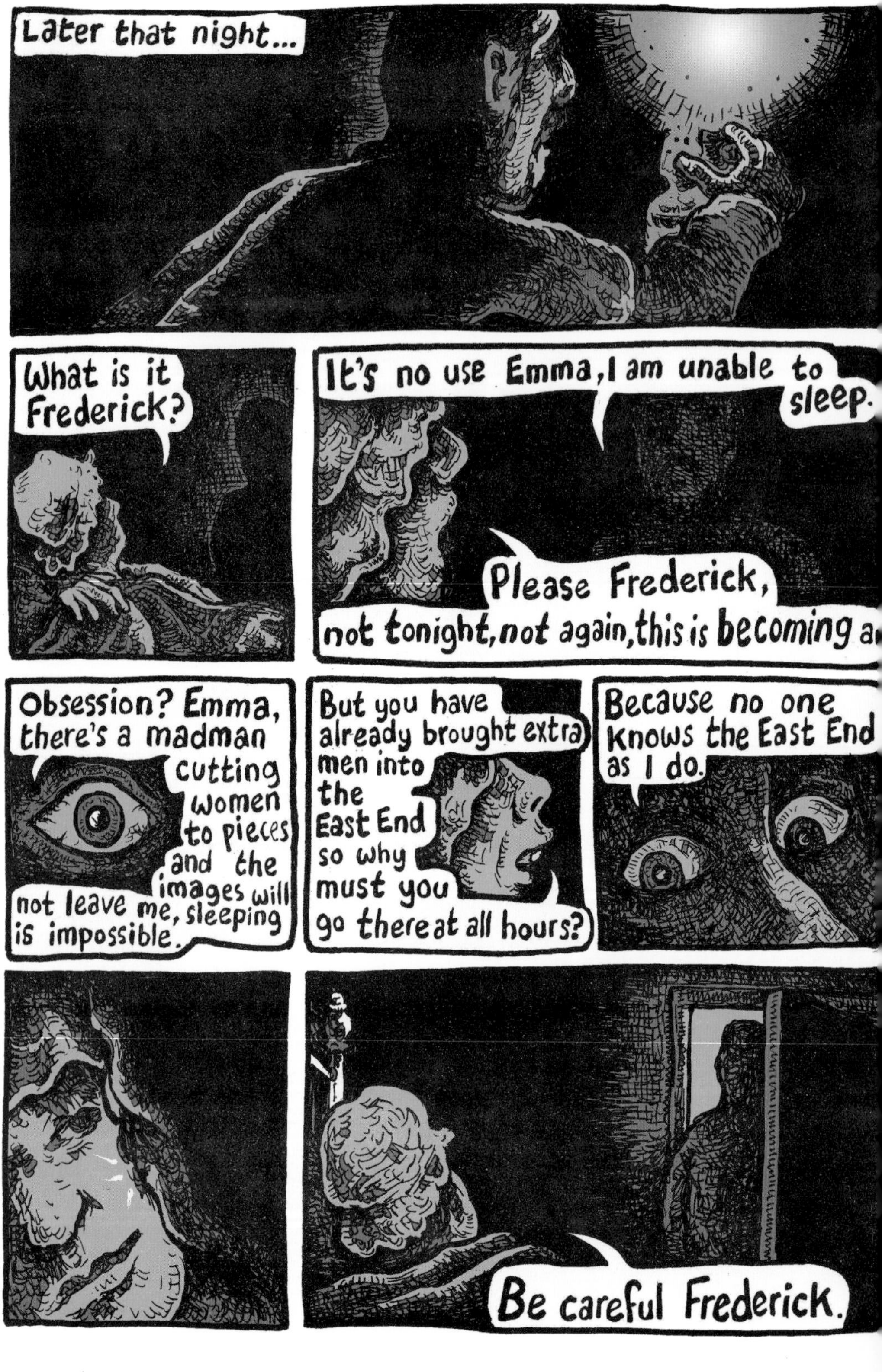
Later that night...
What is it Frederick?
It's no use Emma, I am unable to sleep.
Please Frederick, not tonight, not again, this is becoming a
Obsession? Emma, there's a madman cutting women to pieces and the images will not leave me, sleeping is impossible.
But you have already brought extra men into the East End so why must you go there at all hours?
Because no one knows the East End as I do.
Be careful Frederick.

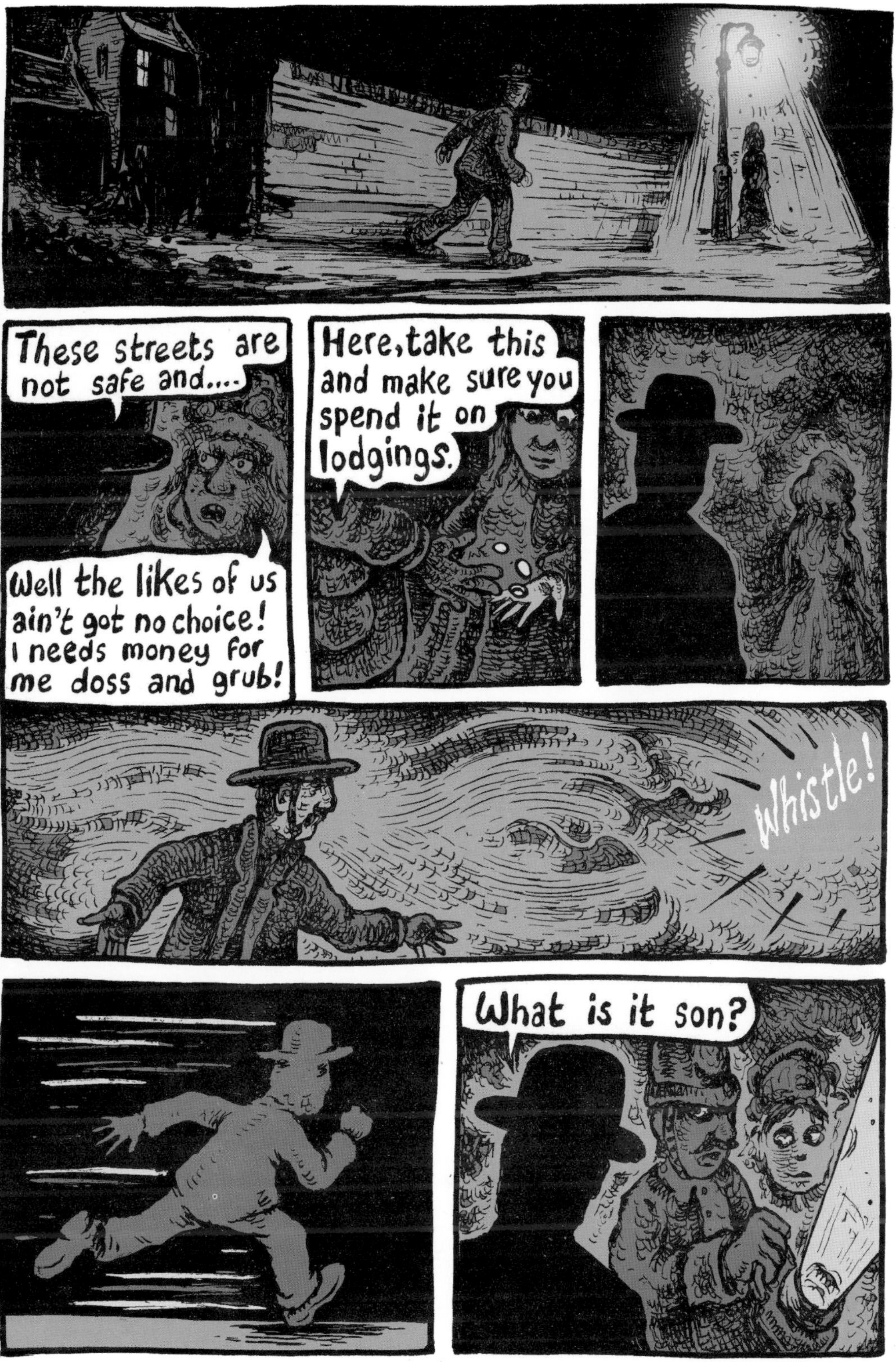
These streets are not safe and....
Well the likes of us ain't got no choice! I needs money for me doss and grub!
Here, take this and make sure you spend it on lodgings.
Whistle!
What is it son?

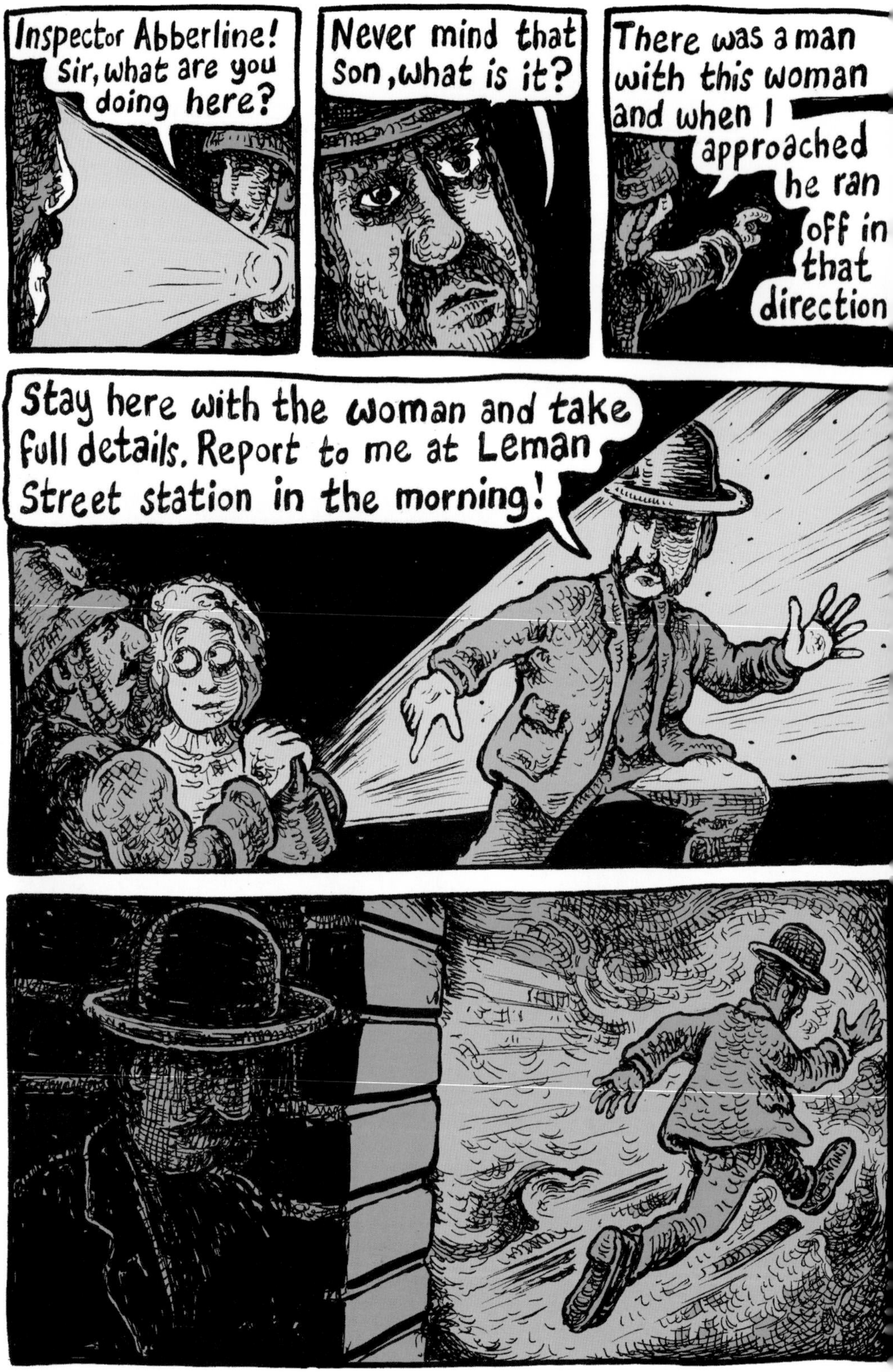
Inspector Abberline! Sir, what are you doing here?
Never mind that son, what is it?
There was a man with this woman and when I approached he ran off in that direction
Stay here with the woman and take full details. Report to me at Leman Street station in the morning!

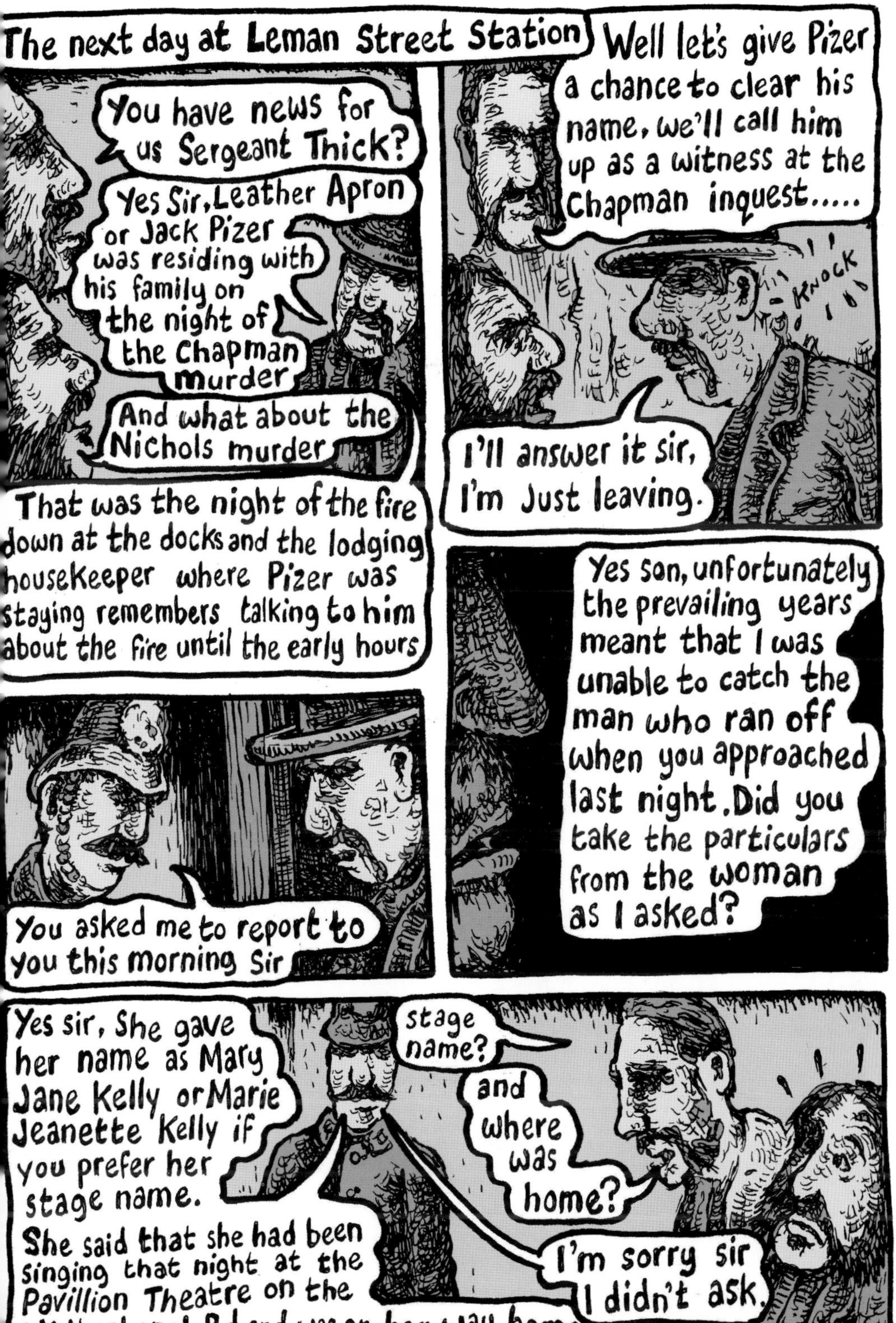
The next day at Leman Street Station
You have news for us Sergeant Thick?
Yes Sir, Leather Apron or Jack Pizer was residing with his family on the night of the Chapman murder
And what about the Nichols murder
That was the night of the fire down at the docks and the lodging houseKeeper where Pizer was staying remembers talking to him about the fire until the early hours
Well let's give Pizer a chance to clear his name, we'll call him up as a witness at the Chapman inquest.....
KNOCK
I'll answer it sir, I'm Just leaving.
You asked me to report to you this morning Sir
Yes son, unfortunately the prevailing years meant that I was unable to catch the man who ran off when you approached last night. Did you take the particulars from the woman as I asked?
Yes sir, She gave her name as Mary Jane Kelly or Marie Jeanette Kelly if you prefer her stage name.
She said that she had been singing that night at the Pavillion Theatre on the Whitechapel Rd and was on her way home
stage name?
and where was home?
I'm sorry sir I didn't ask.

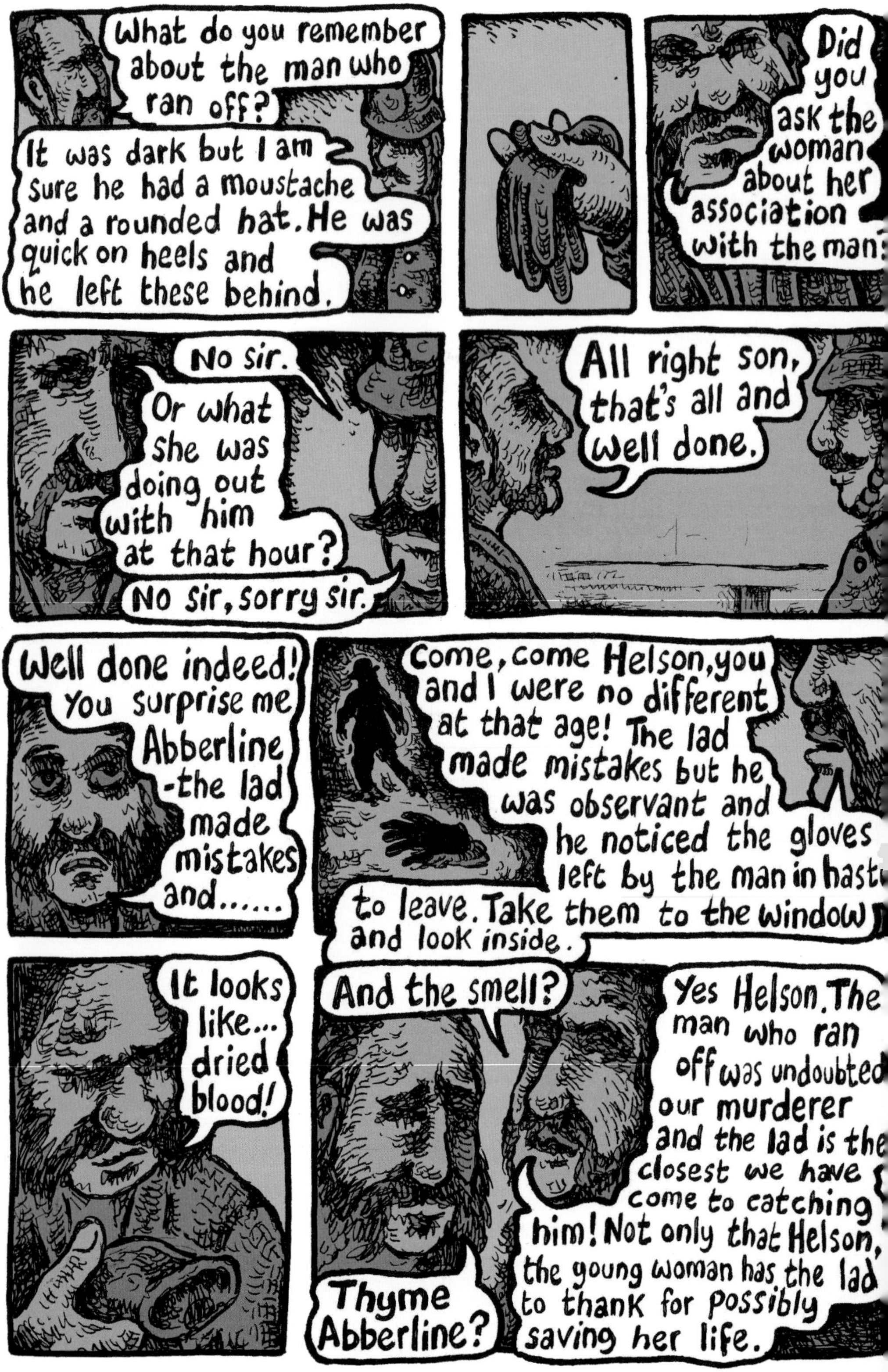
What do you remember about the man who ran off?
It was dark but I am sure he had a moustache and a rounded hat. He was quick on heels and he left these behind.
Did you ask the woman about her association with the man?
No sir.
Or what she was doing out with him at that hour?
No sir, sorry sir.
All right son, that's all and well done.
Well done indeed! You surprise me Abberline -the lad made mistakes and......
Come, come Helson, you and I were no different at that age! The lad made mistakes but he was observant and he noticed the gloves left by the man in haste to leave. Take them to the window and look inside.
It looks like... dried blood!
And the smell?
Thyme Abberline?
Yes Helson. The man who ran off was undoubtedly our murderer and the lad is the closest we have come to catching him! Not only that Helson, the young woman has the lad to thank for possibly saving her life.

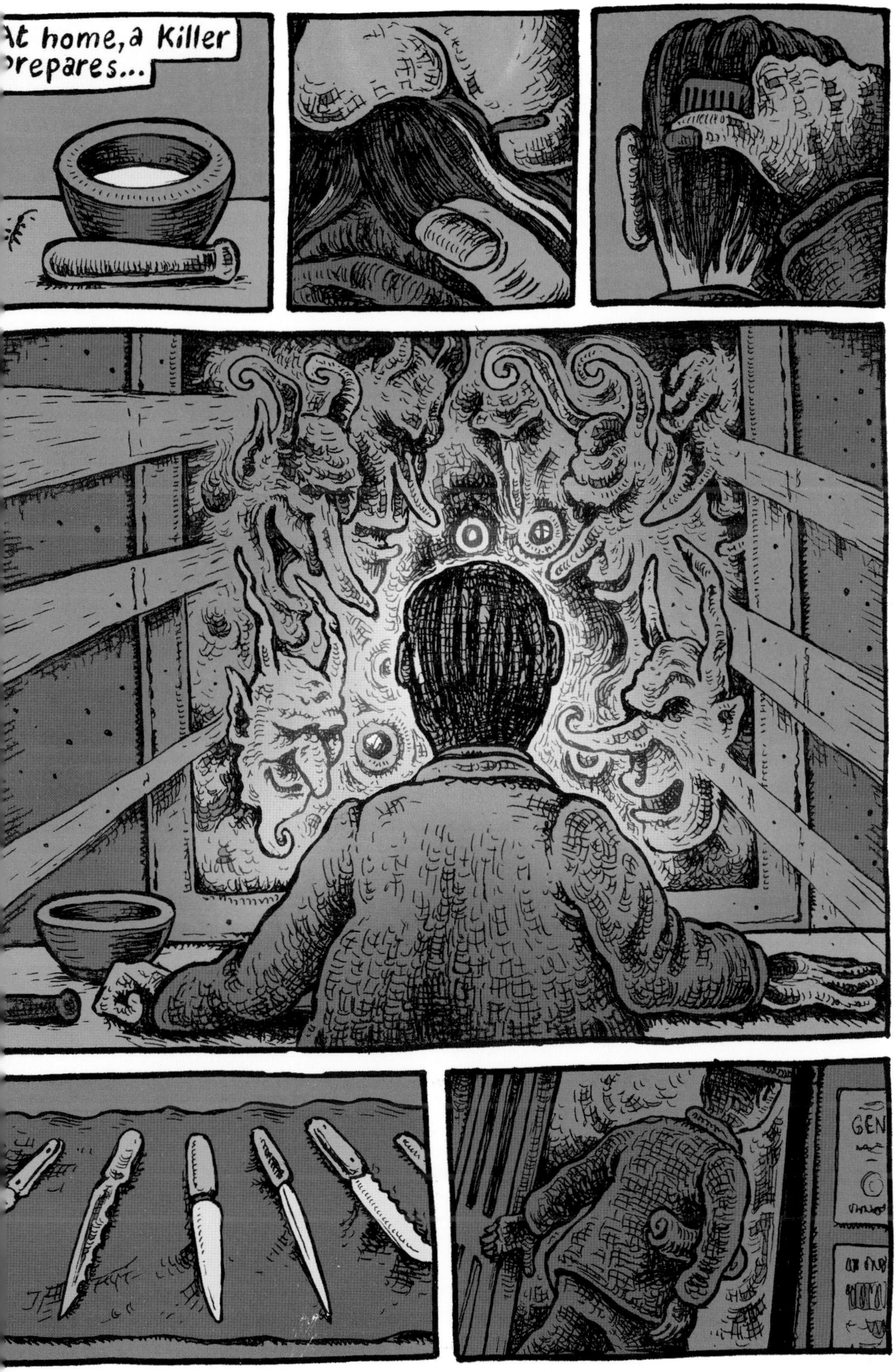
At home,a Killer prepares...
GEN

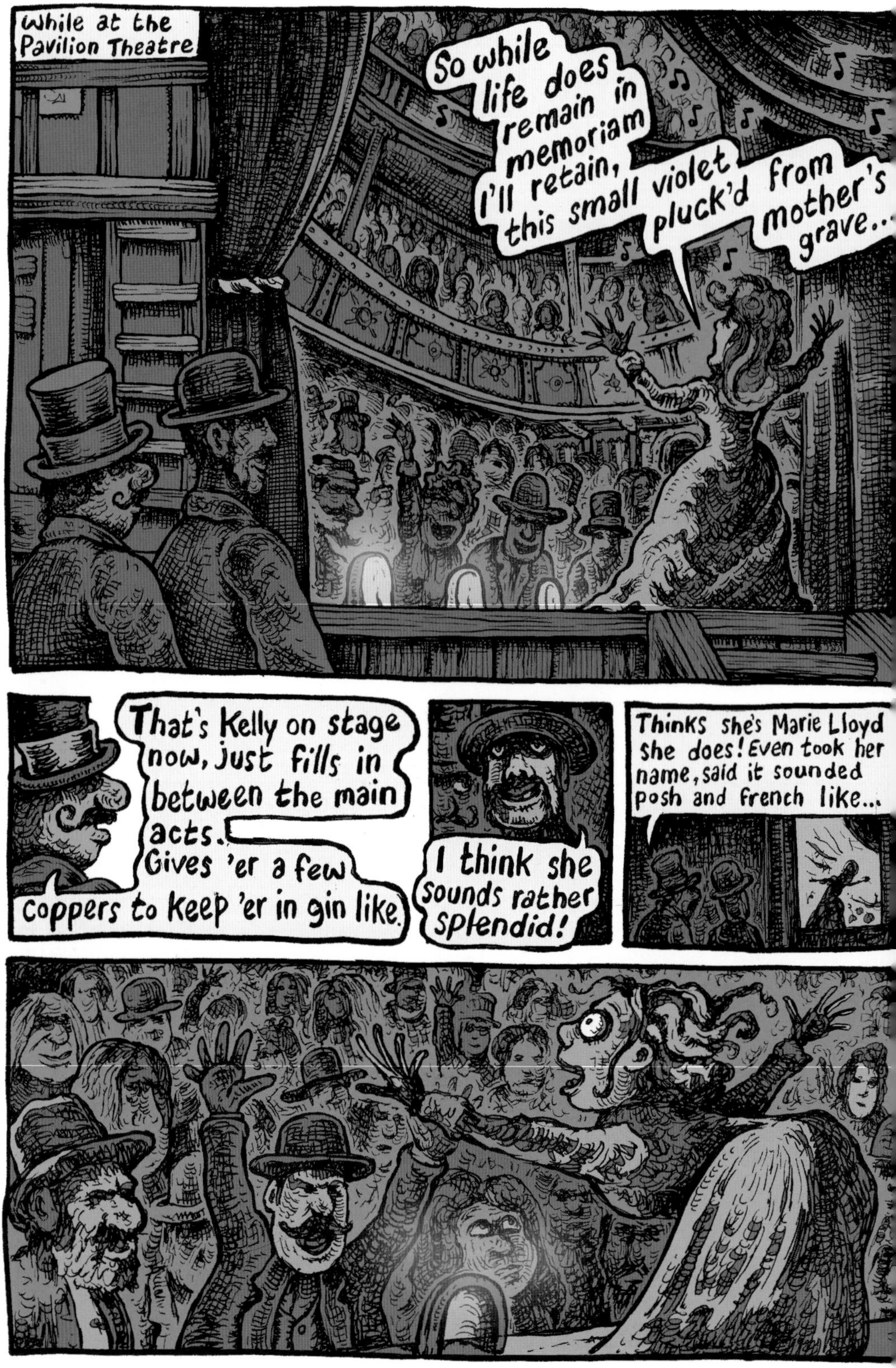
While at the Pavilion Theatre
So while life does remain in memoriam I'll retain, this small violet pluck'd from mother's grave...
That's Kelly on stage now, just fills in between the main acts.
Gives 'er a few coppers to keep 'er in gin like.
I think she sounds rather splendid!
Thinks she's Marie Lloyd she does! Even took her name, said it sounded posh and french like...

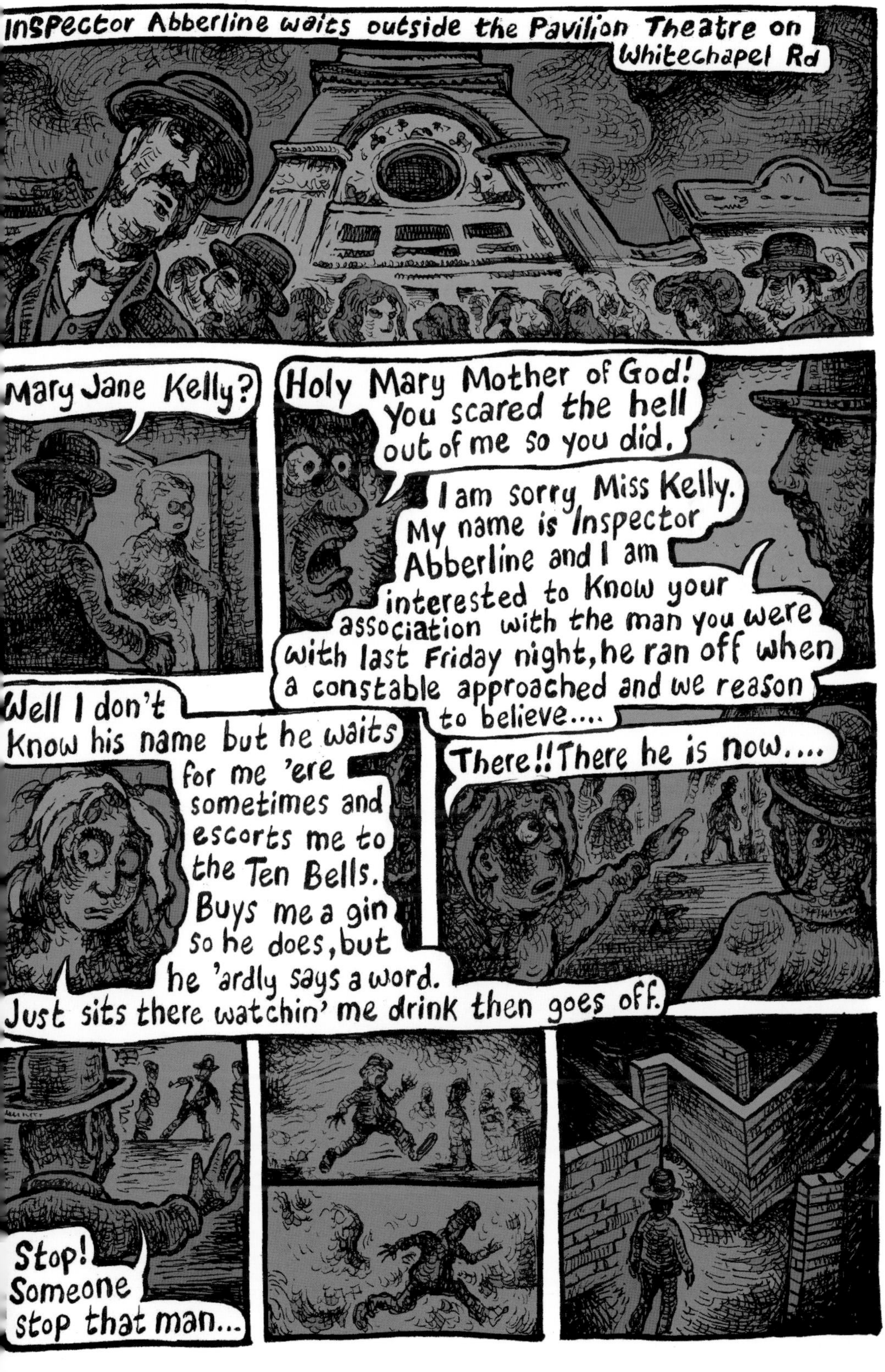
Inspector Abberline waits outside the Pavilion Theatre on Whitechapel Rd
Mary Jane Kelly?
Holy Mary Mother of God! You scared the hell out of me so you did.
I am sorry Miss Kelly. My name is Inspector Abberline and I am interested to Know your association with the man you were with last Friday night, he ran off when a constable approached and we reason to believe....
Well I don't Know his name but he waits for me 'ere sometimes and escorts me to the Ten Bells. Buys me a gin so he does, but he 'ardly says a word. Just sits there watchin' me drink then goes off.
There!! There he is now....
Stop! Someone stop that man...

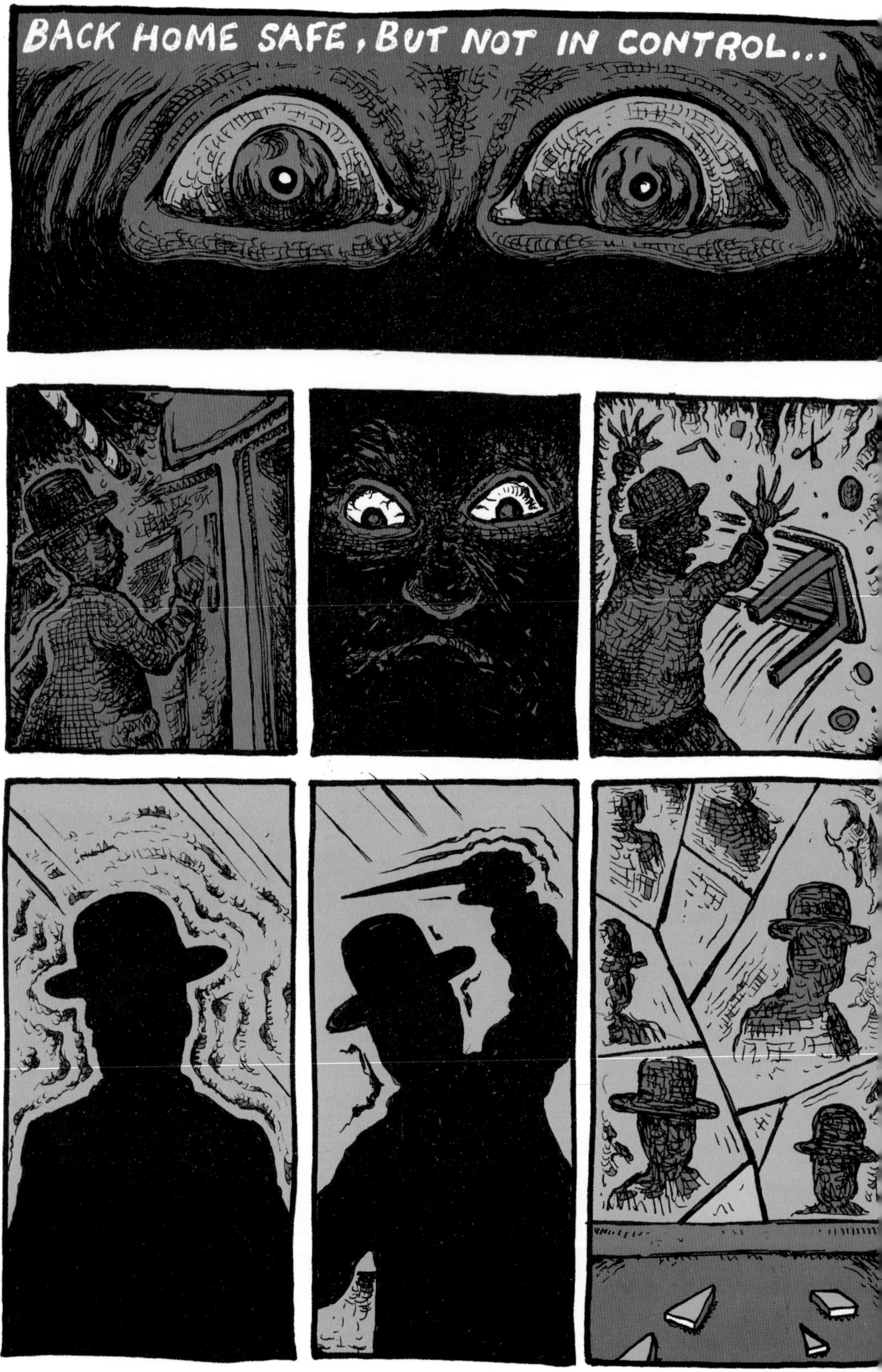
BACK HOME SAFE, BUT NOT IN CONTROL...

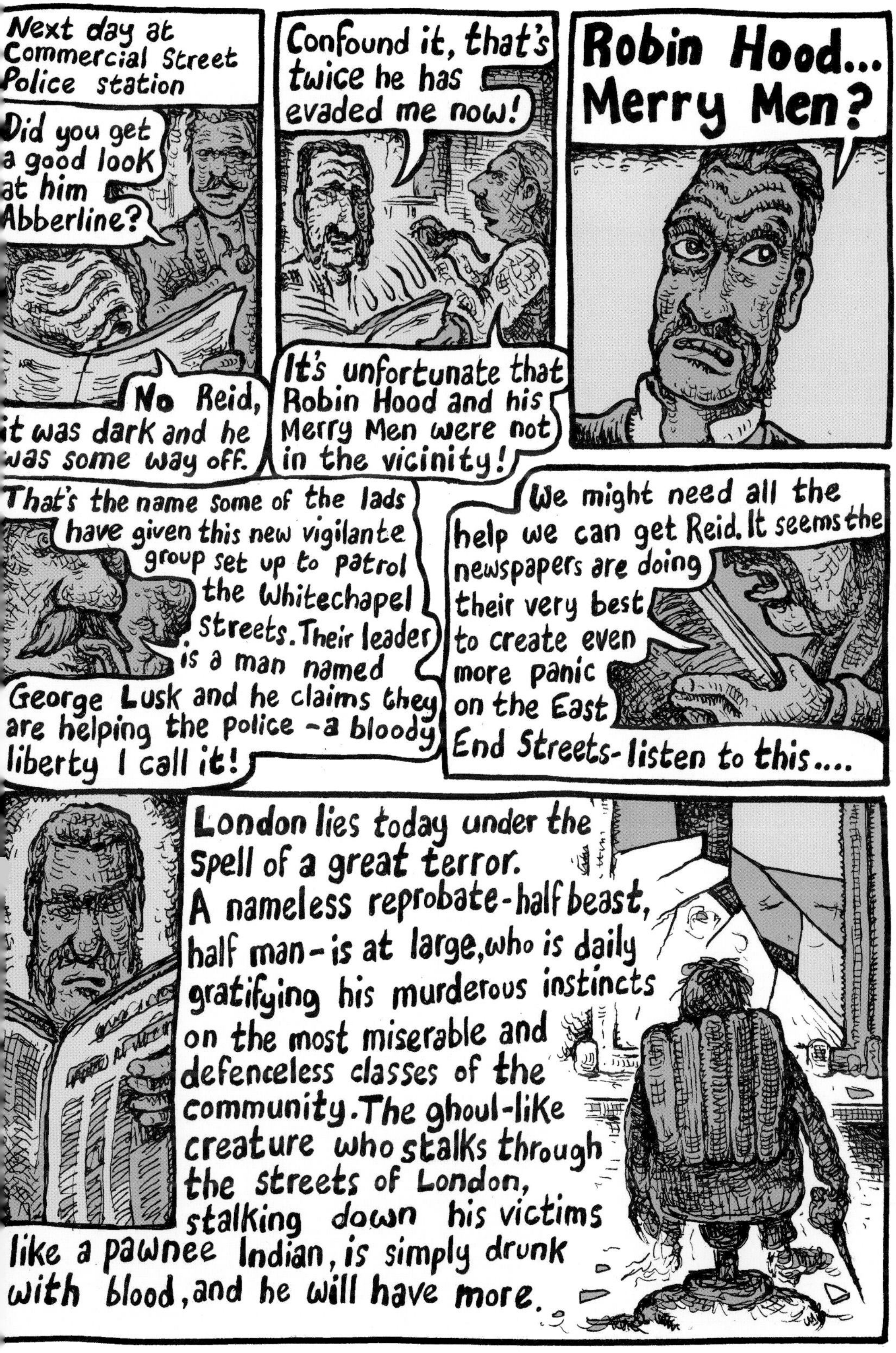
Next day at Commercial Street Police station
Did you get a good look at him Abberline?
No Reid, it was dark and he was some way off.
Confound it, that's twice he has evaded me now!
It's unfortunate that Robin Hood and his Merry Men were not in the vicinity!
Robin Hood... Merry Men?
That's the name some of the lads have given this new vigilante group set up to patrol the Whitechapel streets. Their leader is a man named George Lusk and he claims they are helping the police - a bloody liberty I call it!
We might need all the help we can get Reid. It seems the newspapers are doing their very best to create even more panic on the East End Streets - listen to this....
London lies today under the spell of a great terror. A nameless reprobate - half beast, half man - is at large, who is daily gratifying his murderous instincts on the most miserable and defenceless classes of the community. The ghoul-like creature who stalks through the streets of London, stalking down his victims like a pawnee Indian, is simply drunk with blood, and he will have more.

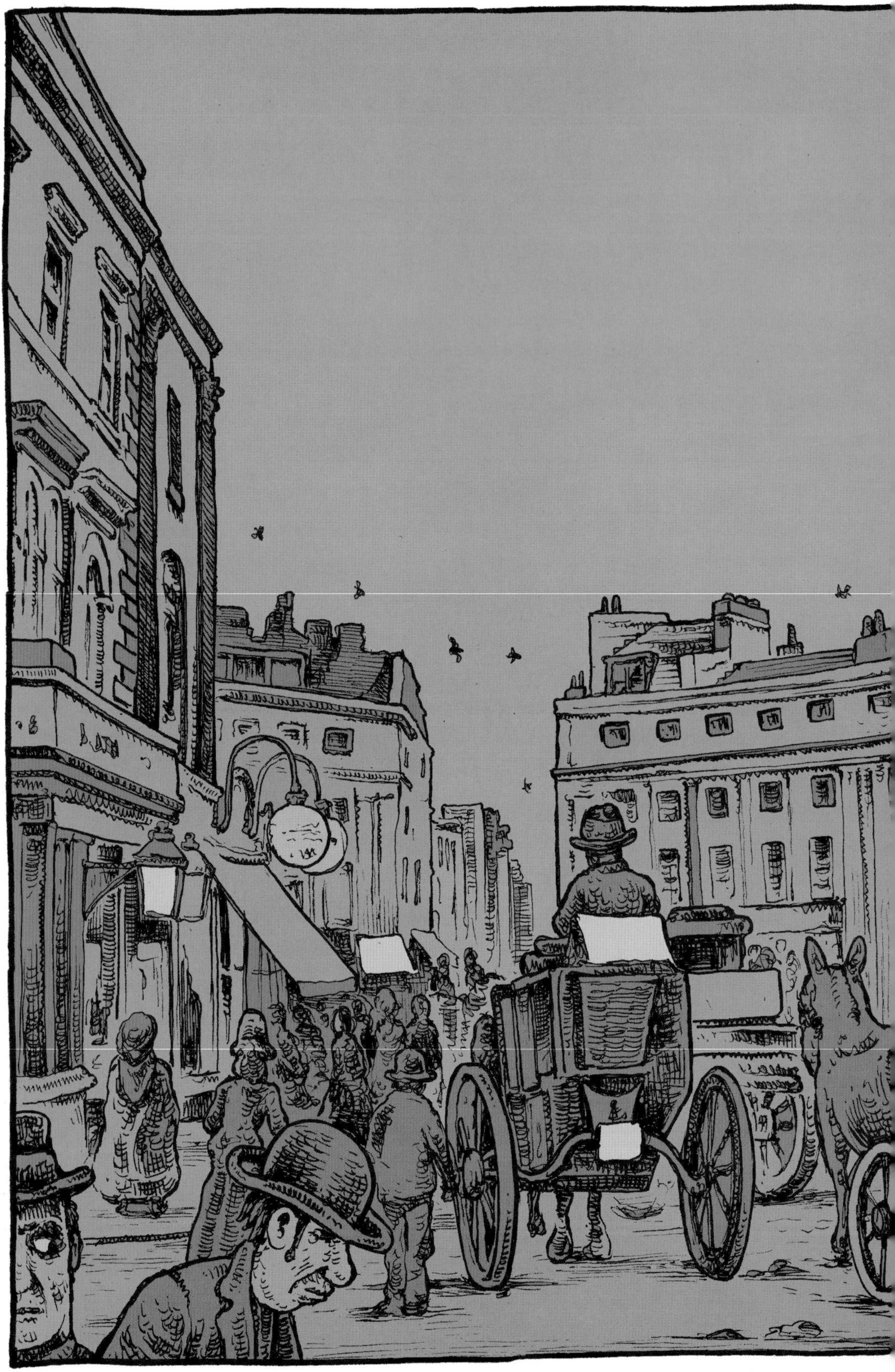

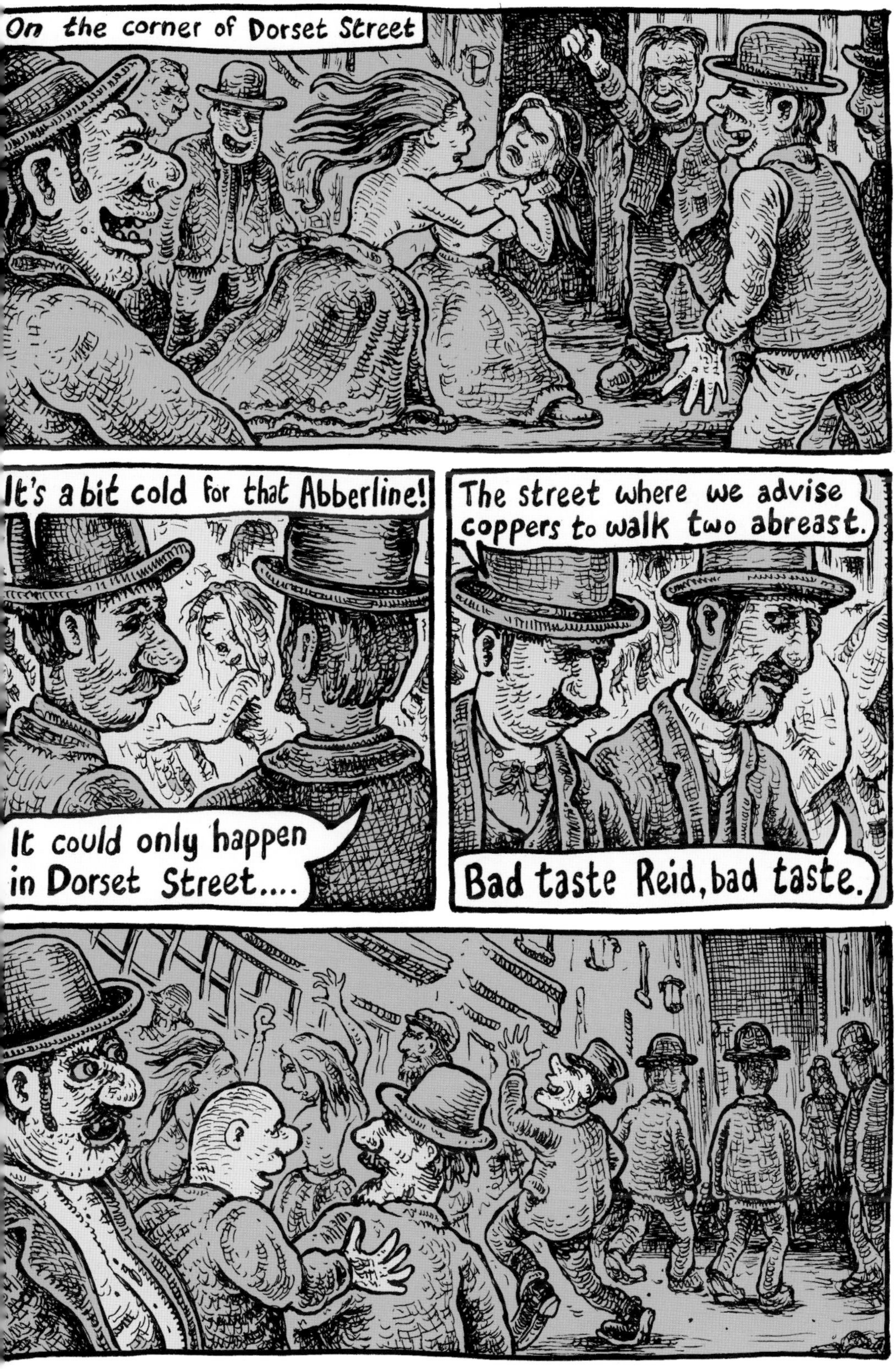
On the corner of Dorset Street
It's a bit cold for that Abberline!
It could only happen in Dorset Street....
The street where we advise coppers to walk two abreast.
Bad taste Reid, bad taste.

But seriously Abberline, it's almost as though nothing ever happened, the East End looks so...normal

Well it's been a while now since the murder of Annie Chapman but the perpetrator is still at large—we must not lose sight of that fact.

THE TEN BELLS

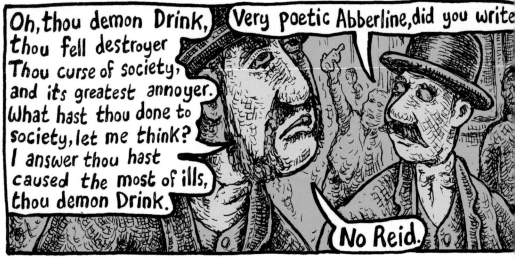

Oh, thou demon Drink, thou fell destroyer Thou curse of society, and its greatest annoyer. What hast thou done to society, let me think? I answer thou hast caused the most of ills, thou demon Drink.

Very poetic Abberline, did you write

No Reid.

commercial st.

Sergeant Thick has filed a report charting the searches of private dwellings and lodging houses.

Good, let us also continue to keep the Pavilion Theatre under observation. We have been unable to trace the woman Kelly and I fear she is in more danger than she realises.

Well you 'ad the bright notion to lug it 'ome! Nice little 'oliday that were, hop pickin' in Kent!

Come on gal, you can't sit on yer arse all day?

Give in ya gabbin' — me feet's still killin' me from that jaunt yesterday.

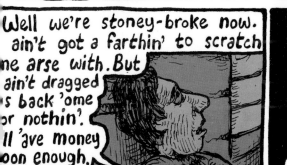

Well we're stoney-broke now. ain't got a farthin' to scratch me arse with. But ain't dragged 's back 'ome or nothin'. ll 'ave money oon enough.

You be careful Kate, do you 'ear me now, be careful...!

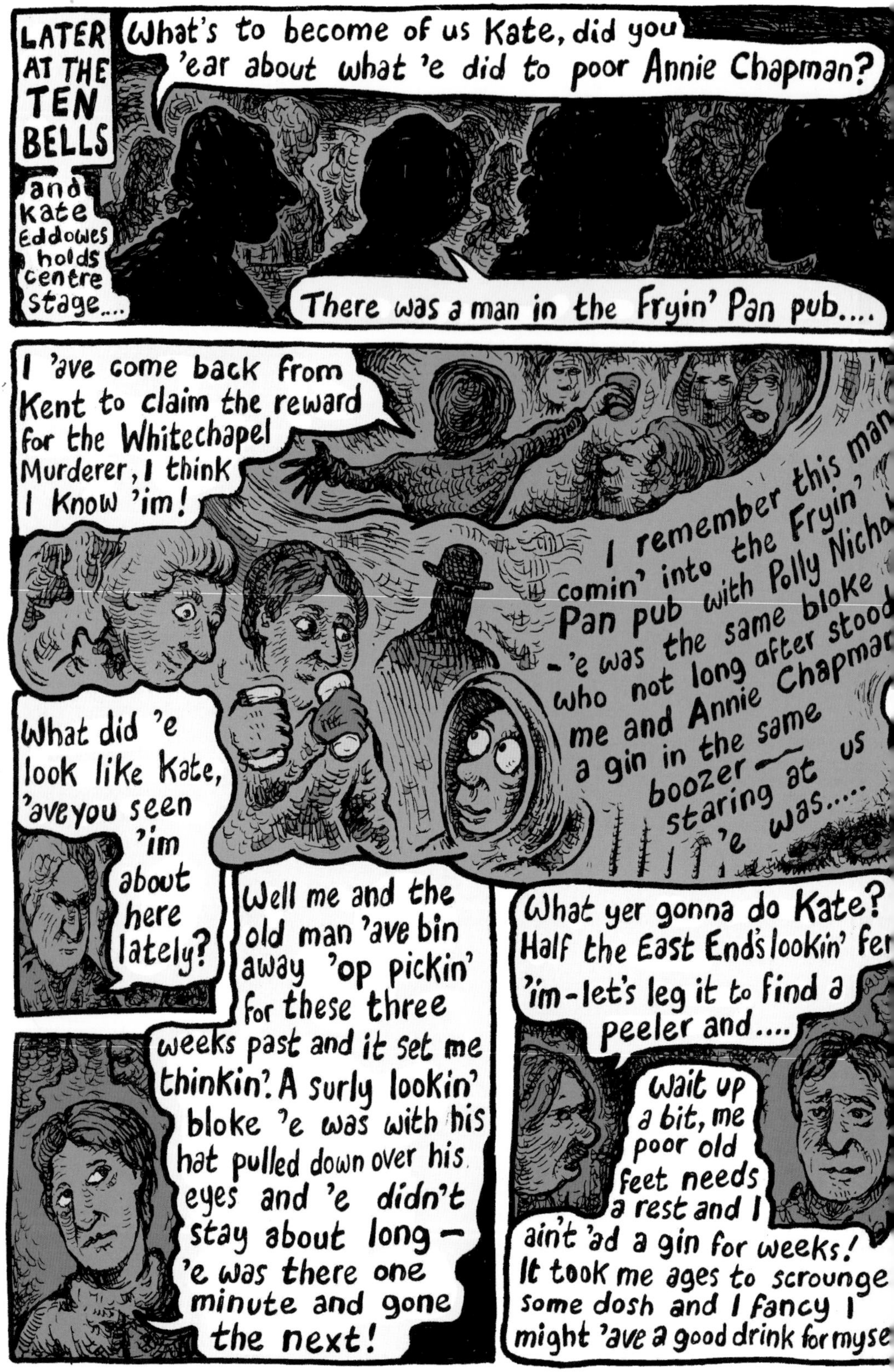

LATER AT THE TEN BELLS
and Kate Eddowes holds centre stage....
What's to become of us Kate, did you 'ear about what 'e did to poor Annie Chapman?
There was a man in the Fryin' Pan pub....
I 'ave come back from Kent to claim the reward for the Whitechapel Murderer, I think I Know 'im!
I remember this man comin' into the Fryin' Pan pub with Polly Nicho
'e was the same bloke - who not long after stood me and Annie Chapman a gin in the same boozer — staring at us 'e was.....
What did 'e look like Kate, 'ave you seen 'im about here lately?
Well me and the old man 'ave bin away 'op pickin' for these three weeks past and it set me thinkin'. A surly lookin' bloke 'e was with his hat pulled down over his eyes and 'e didn't stay about long — 'e was there one minute and gone the next!
What yer gonna do Kate? Half the East End's lookin' fer 'im - let's leg it to find a peeler and....
Wait up a bit, me poor old feet needs a rest and I ain't 'ad a gin for weeks! It took me ages to scrounge some dosh and I fancy I might 'ave a good drink for myse

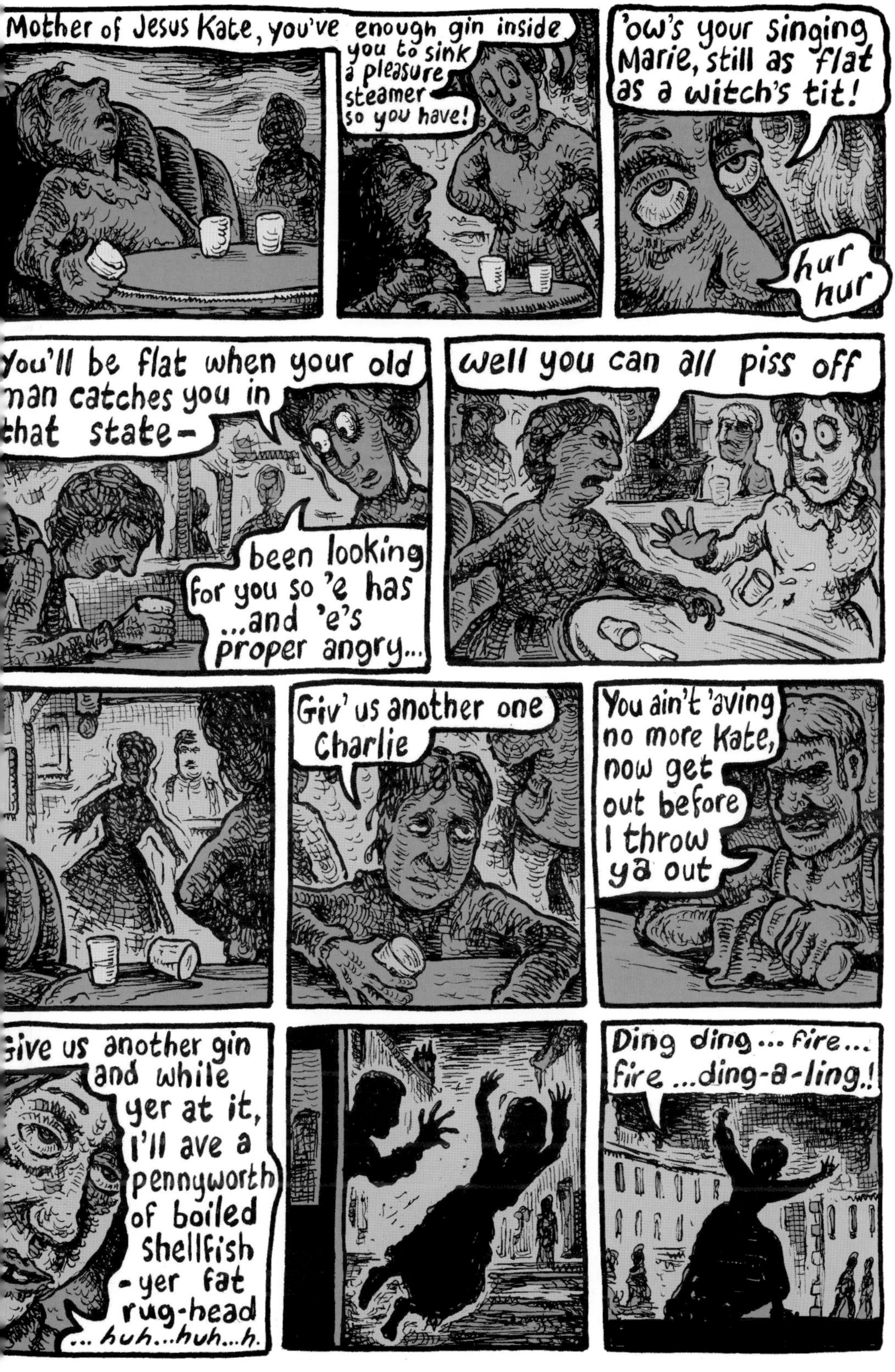

Mother of Jesus Kate, you've enough gin inside you to sink a pleasure steamer so you have!
'ow's your singing Marie, still as flat as a witch's tit!
hur hur
You'll be flat when your old man catches you in that state-
been looking for you so 'e has ...and 'e's proper angry...
well you can all piss off
Giv' us another one Charlie
You ain't 'aving no more Kate, now get out before I throw ya out
Give us another gin and while yer at it, I'll ave a pennyworth of boiled shellfish - yer fat rug-head ... huh...huh...h.
Ding ding... fire... fire ...ding-a-ling.!

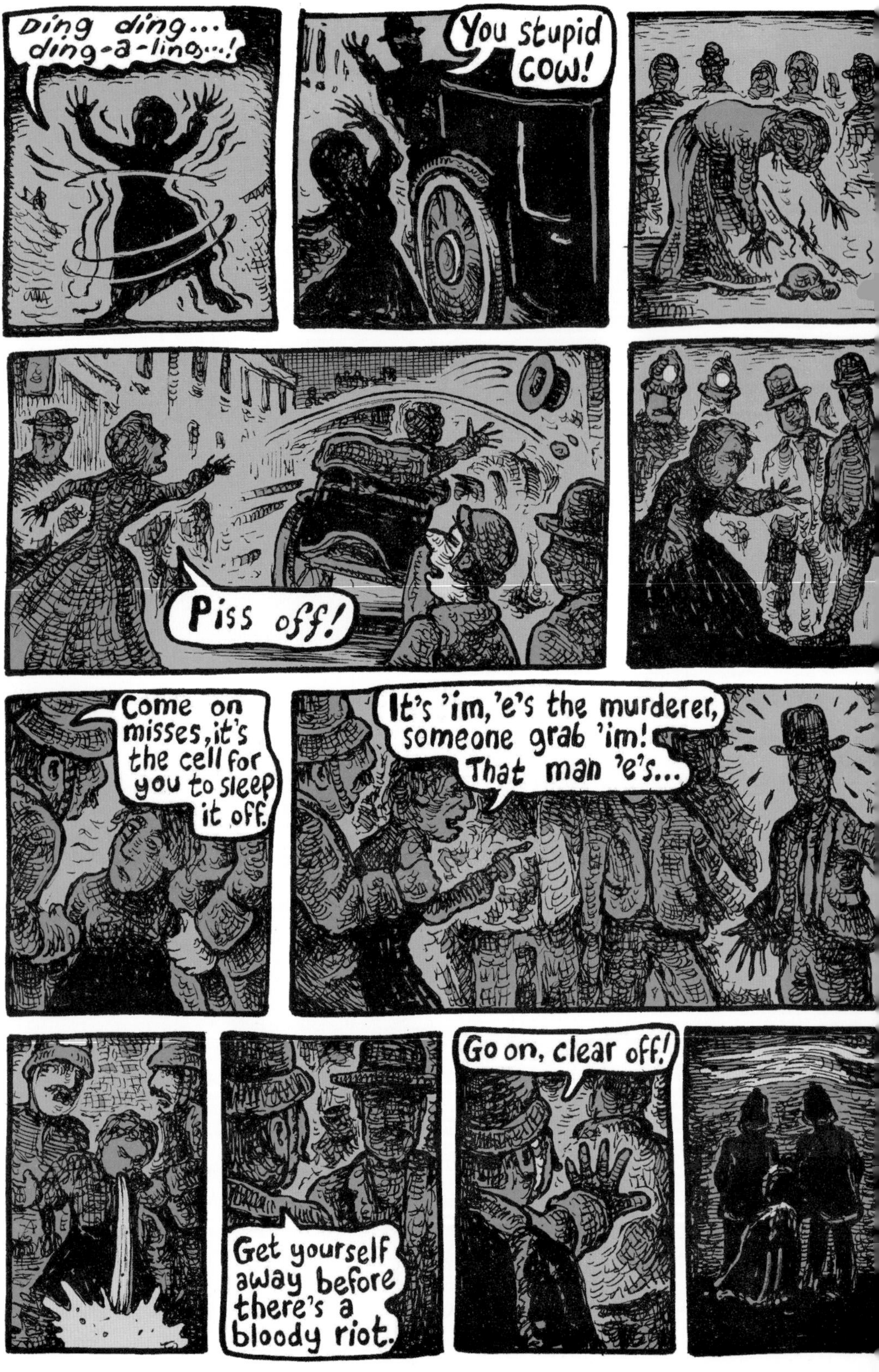
Ding ding...
ding-a-ling...!
You stupid cow!
Piss off!
Come on misses, it's the cell for you to sleep it off.
It's 'im, 'e's the murderer, someone grab 'im! That man 'e's...
Get yourself away before there's a bloody riot.
Go on, clear off!

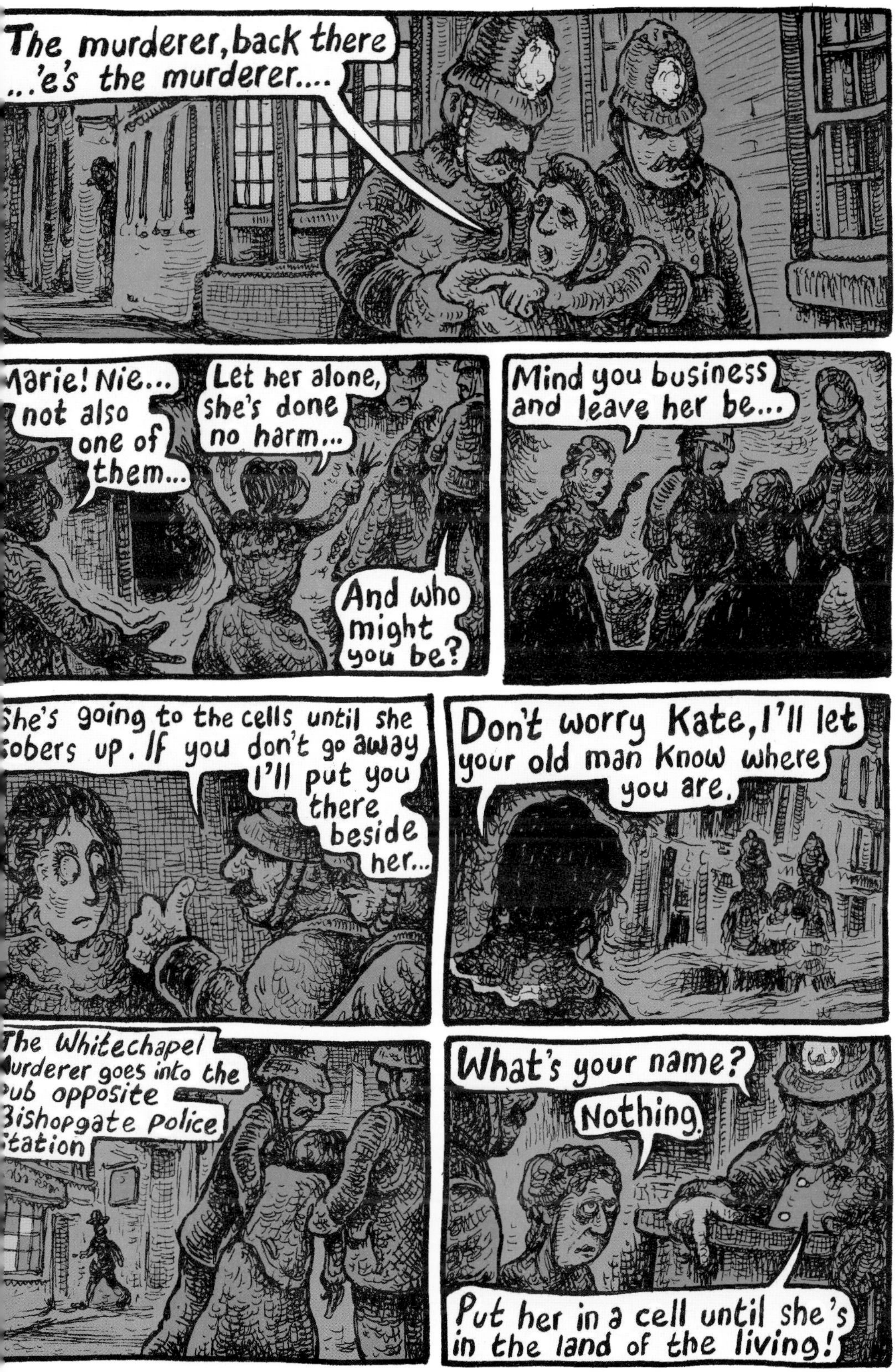
The murderer, back there ...'e's the murderer....
Marie! Nie... not also one of them...
Let her alone, she's done no harm...
And who might you be?
Mind you business and leave her be...
She's going to the cells until she sobers up. If you don't go away I'll put you there beside her...
Don't worry Kate, I'll let your old man know where you are.
The Whitechapel Murderer goes into the pub opposite Bishopgate Police Station
What's your name?
Nothing.
Put her in a cell until she's in the land of the living!

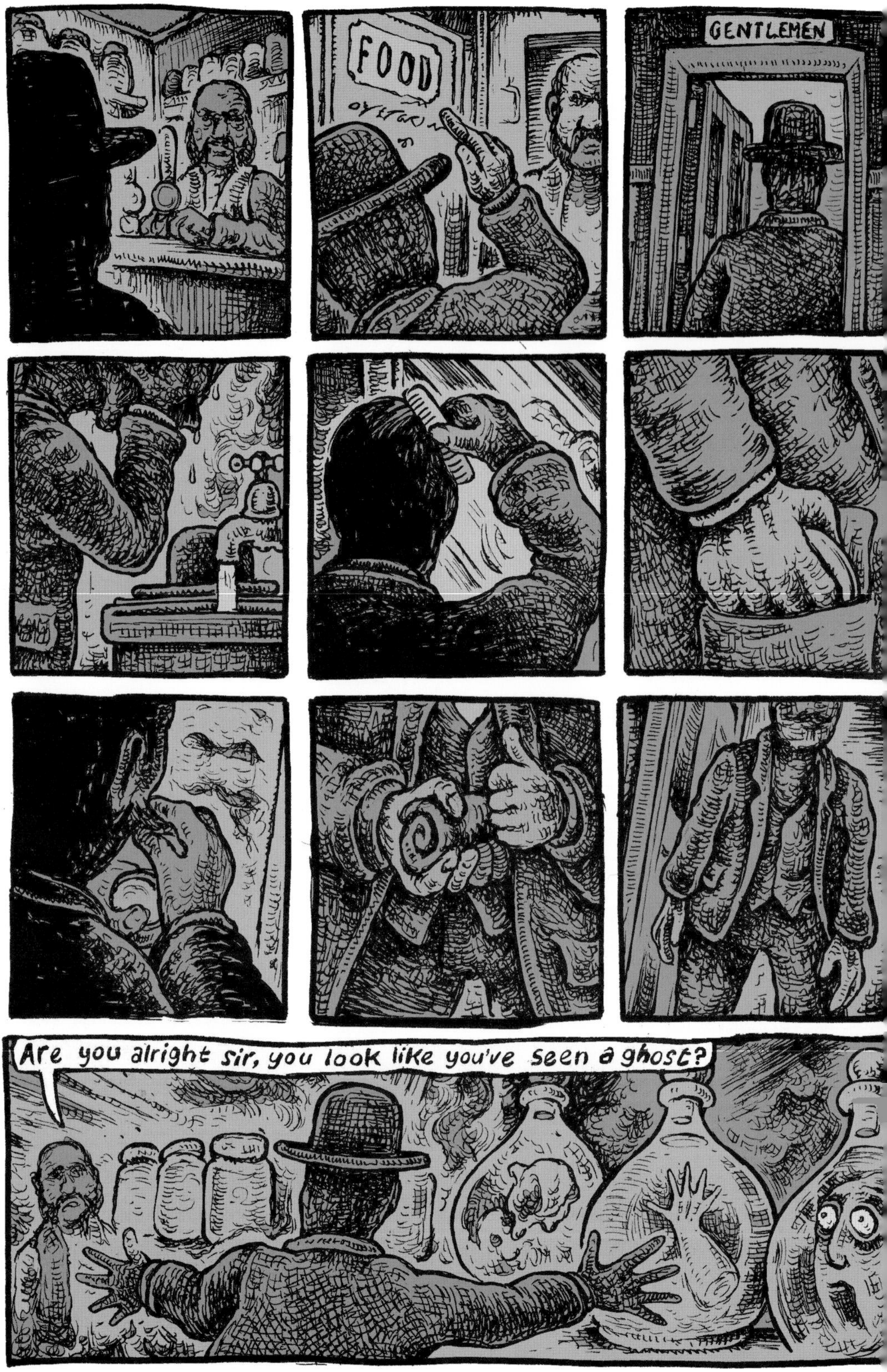
FOOD
GENTLEMEN
Are you alright sir, you look like you've seen a ghost?

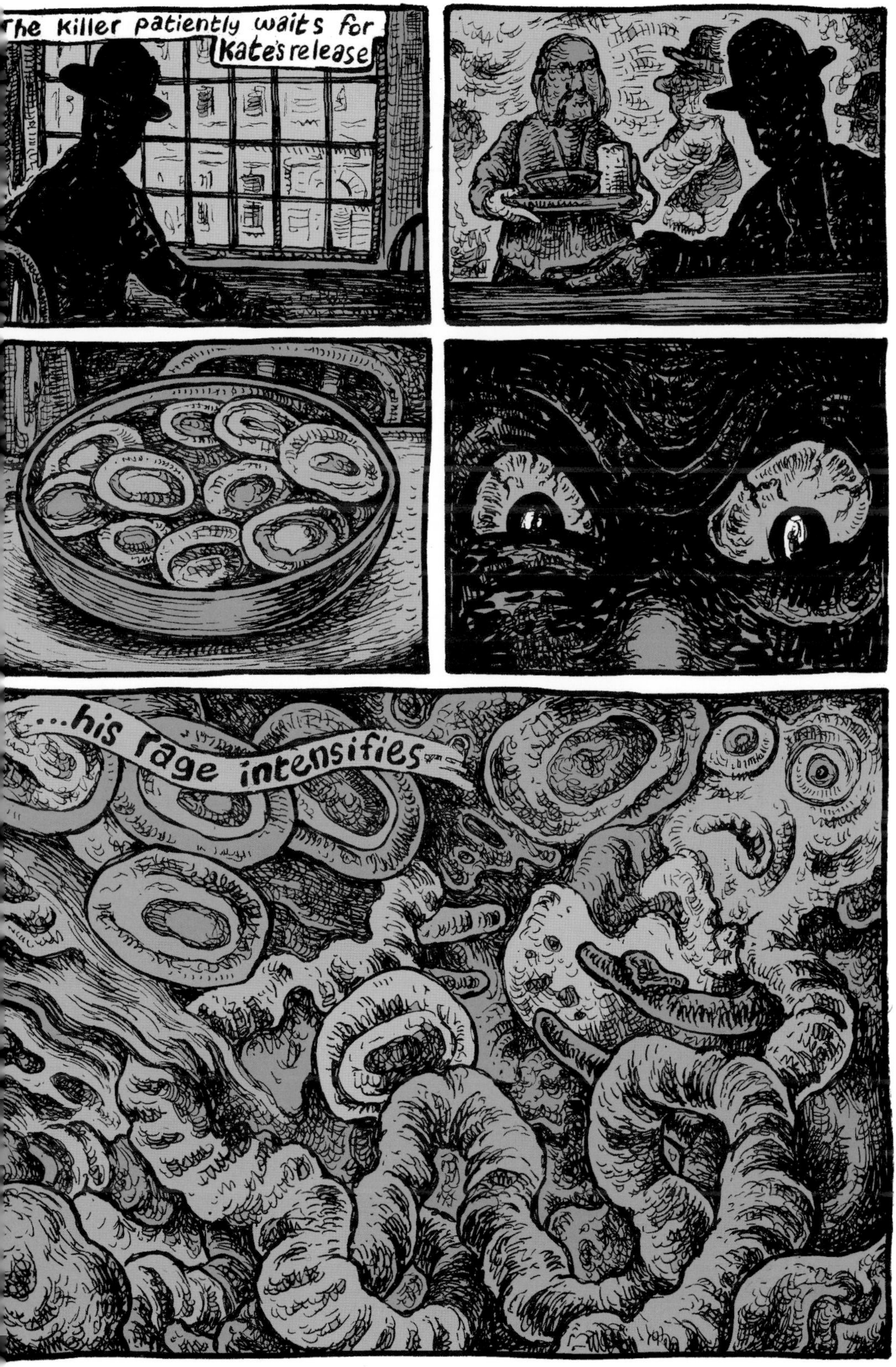
The killer patiently waits for Kate's release
...his rage intensifies

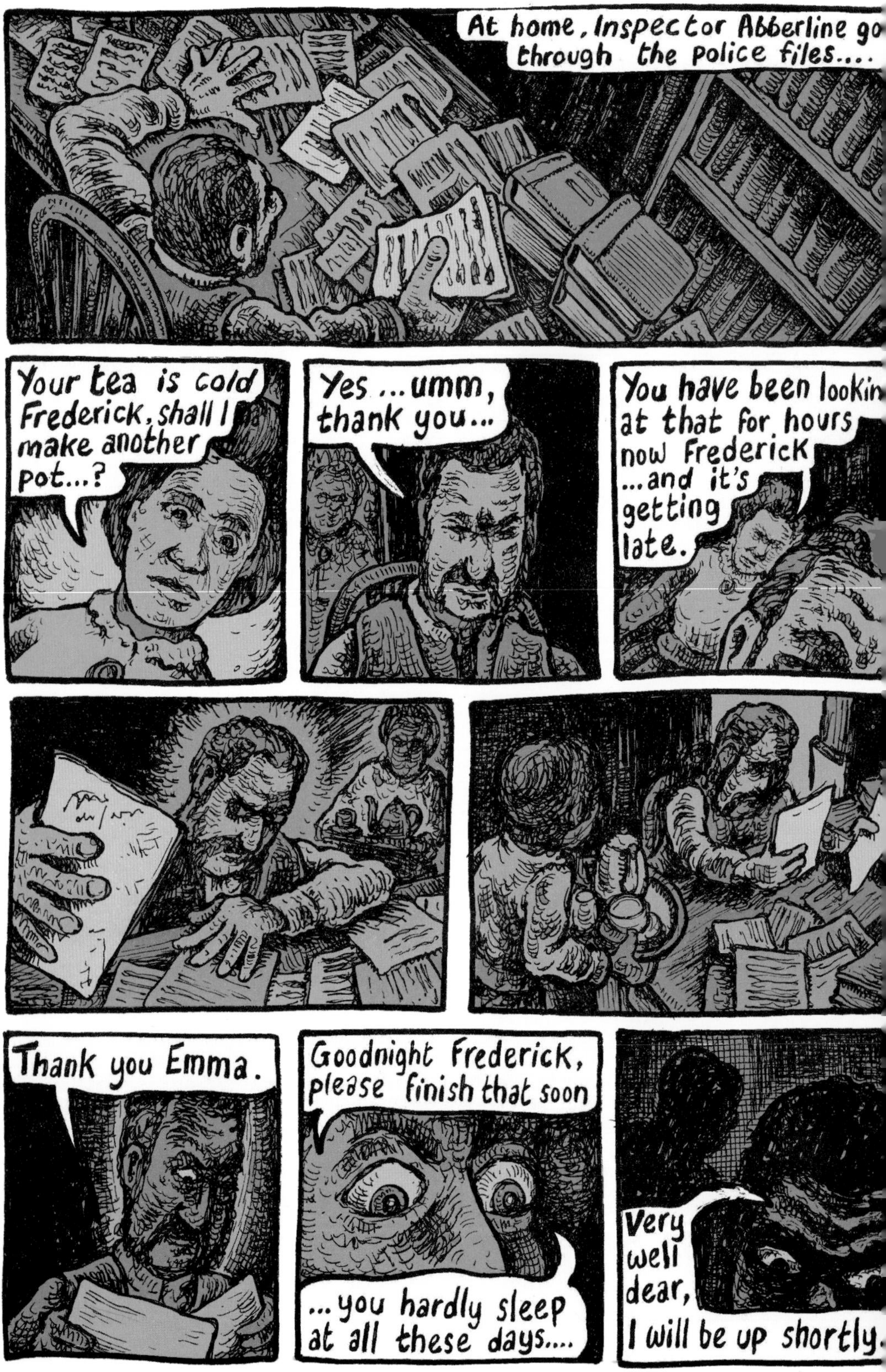
At home, Inspector Abberline go
through the police files....
Your tea is cold Frederick, shall I make another pot...?
Yes ... umm, thank you...
You have been lookin
at that for hours now Frederick ...and it's getting late.
Thank you Emma.
Goodnight Frederick, please finish that soon
...you hardly sleep at all these days....
Very well dear,
I will be up shortly.

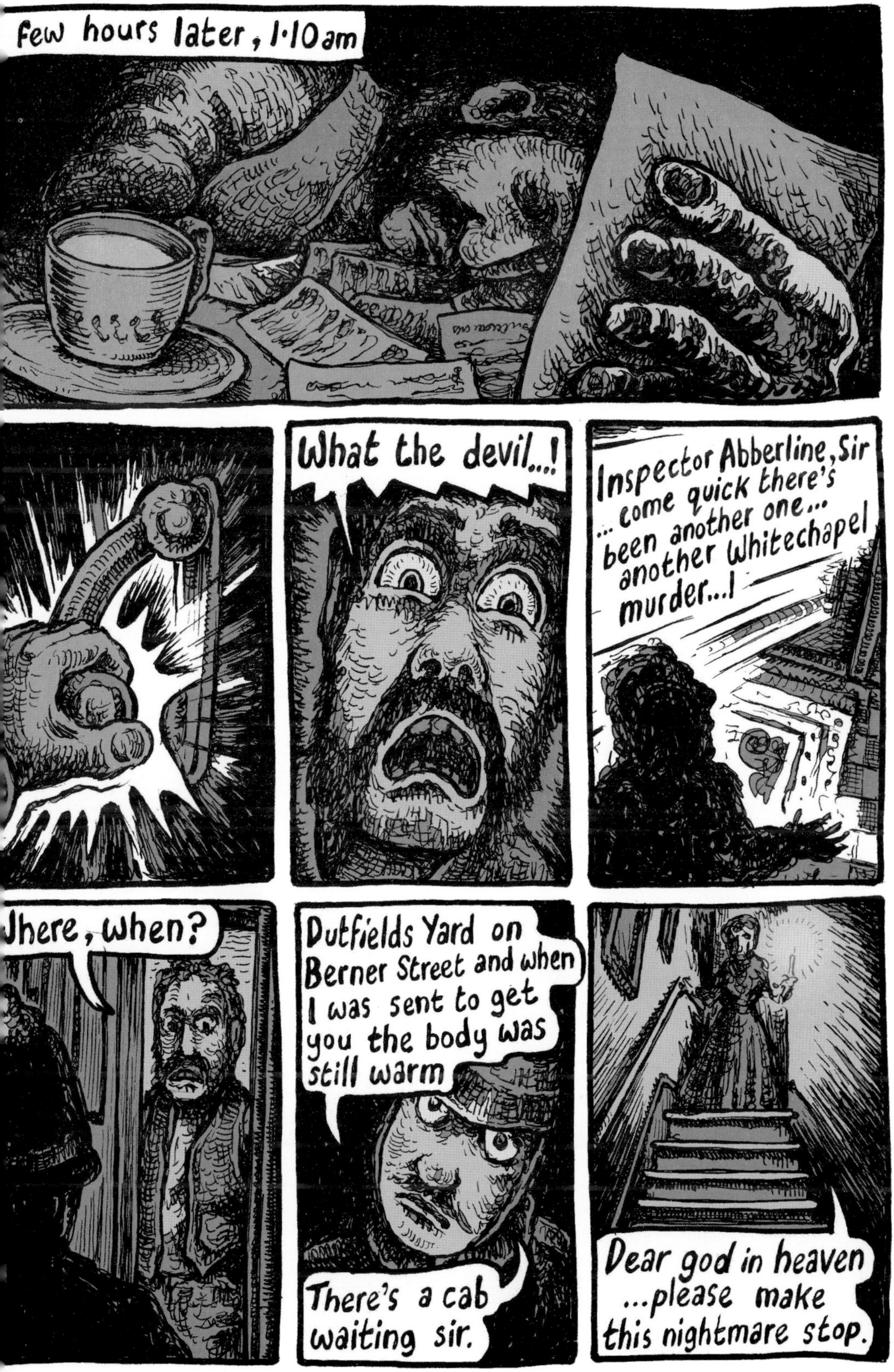
Few hours later, 1·10am
What the devil...!
Inspector Abberline, Sir ... come quick there's been another one... another Whitechapel murder...!
Where, when?
Dutfields Yard on Berner Street and when I was sent to get you the body was still warm
There's a cab waiting sir.
Dear god in heaven ...please make this nightmare stop.

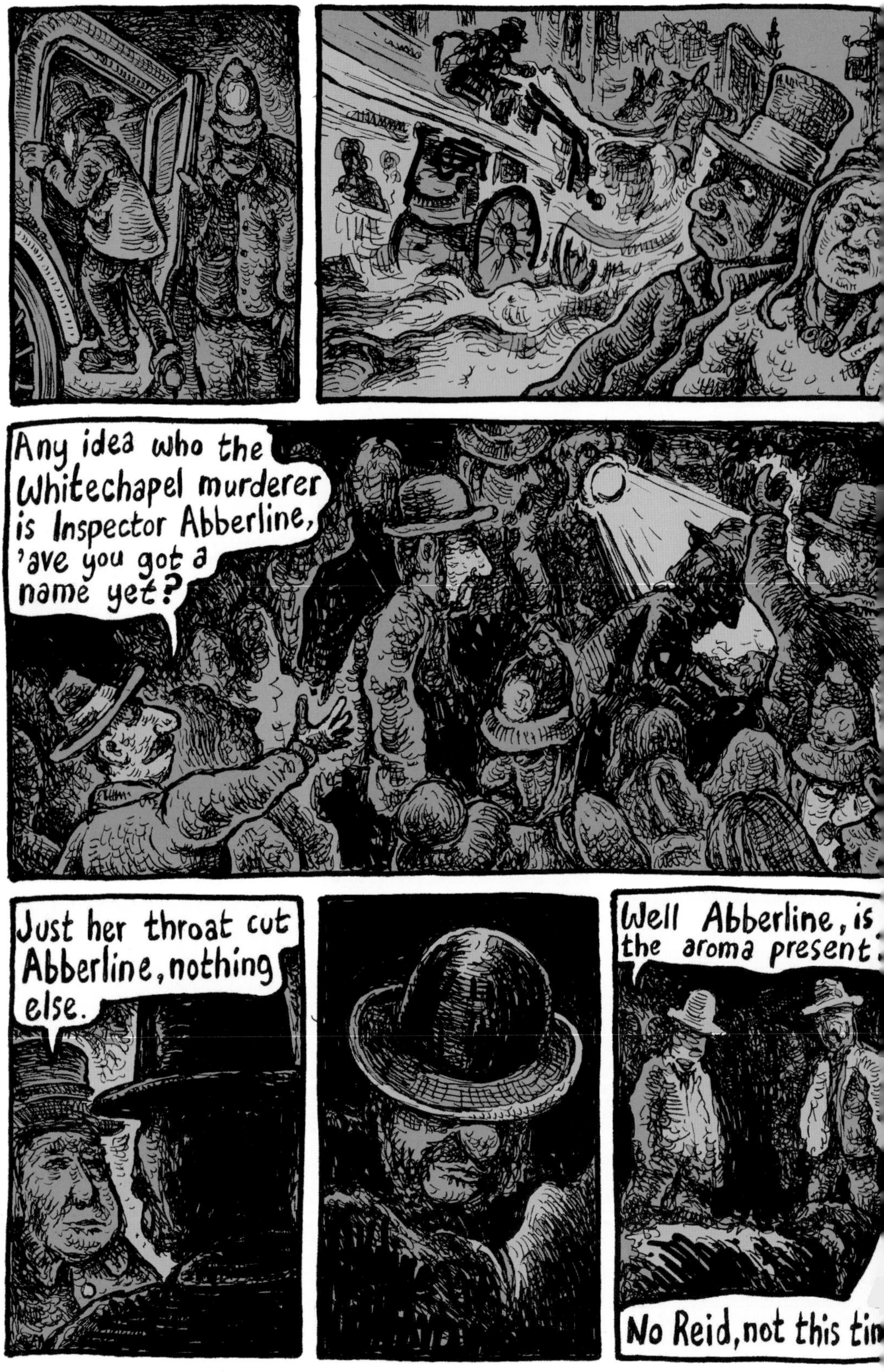
Any idea who the Whitechapel murderer is Inspector Abberline, 'ave you got a name yet?
Just her throat cut Abberline, nothing else.
Well Abberline, is the aroma present?
No Reid, not this tim

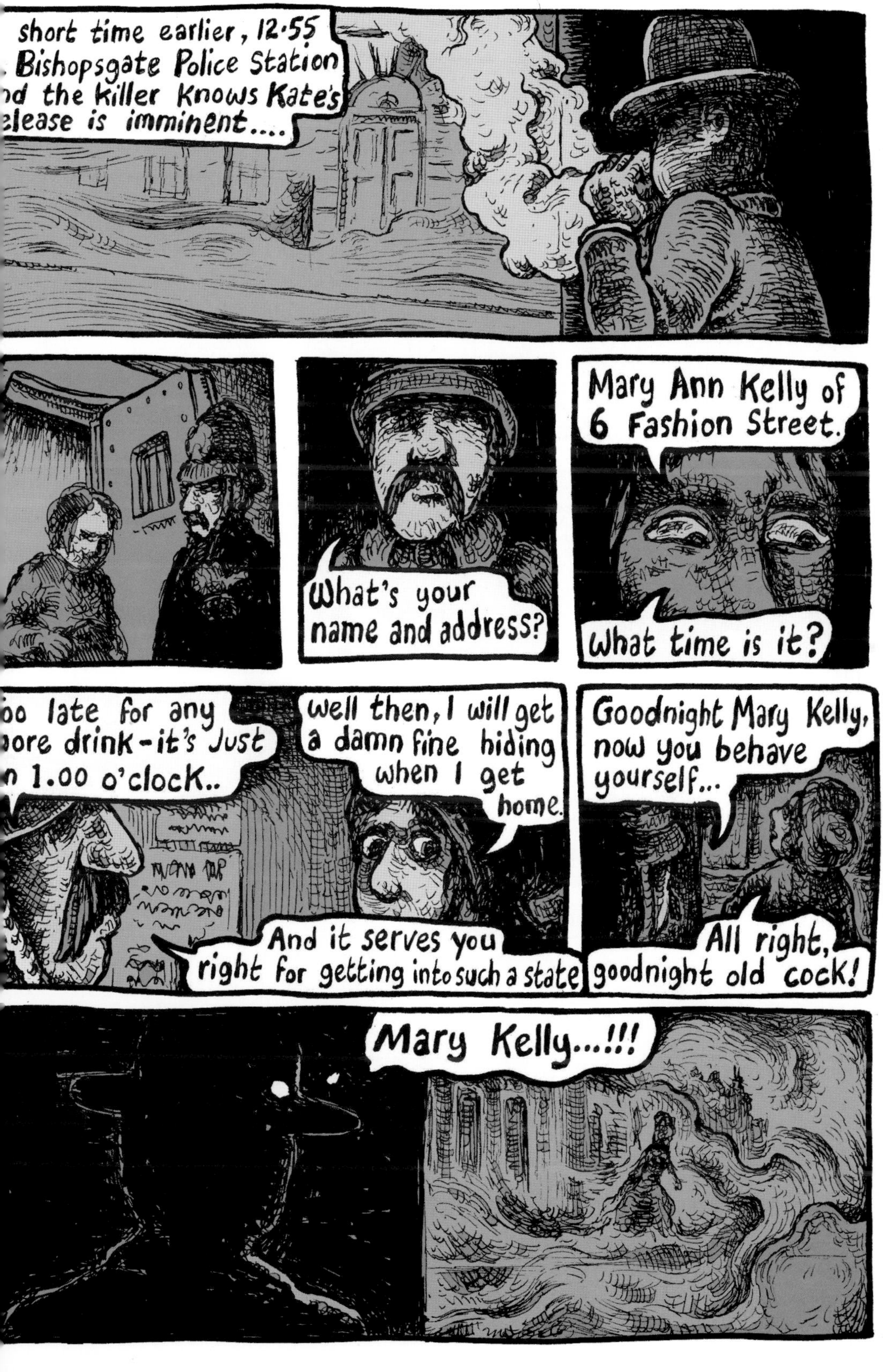
short time earlier, 12·55
Bishopsgate Police Station
nd the killer knows Kate's
elease is imminent....
What's your name and address?
Mary Ann Kelly of 6 Fashion Street.
What time is it?
oo late for any ore drink - it's just n 1.00 o'clock..
well then, I will get a damn fine hiding when I get home.
And it serves you right for getting into such a state
Goodnight Mary Kelly, now you behave yourself...
All right, goodnight old cock!
Mary Kelly...!!!

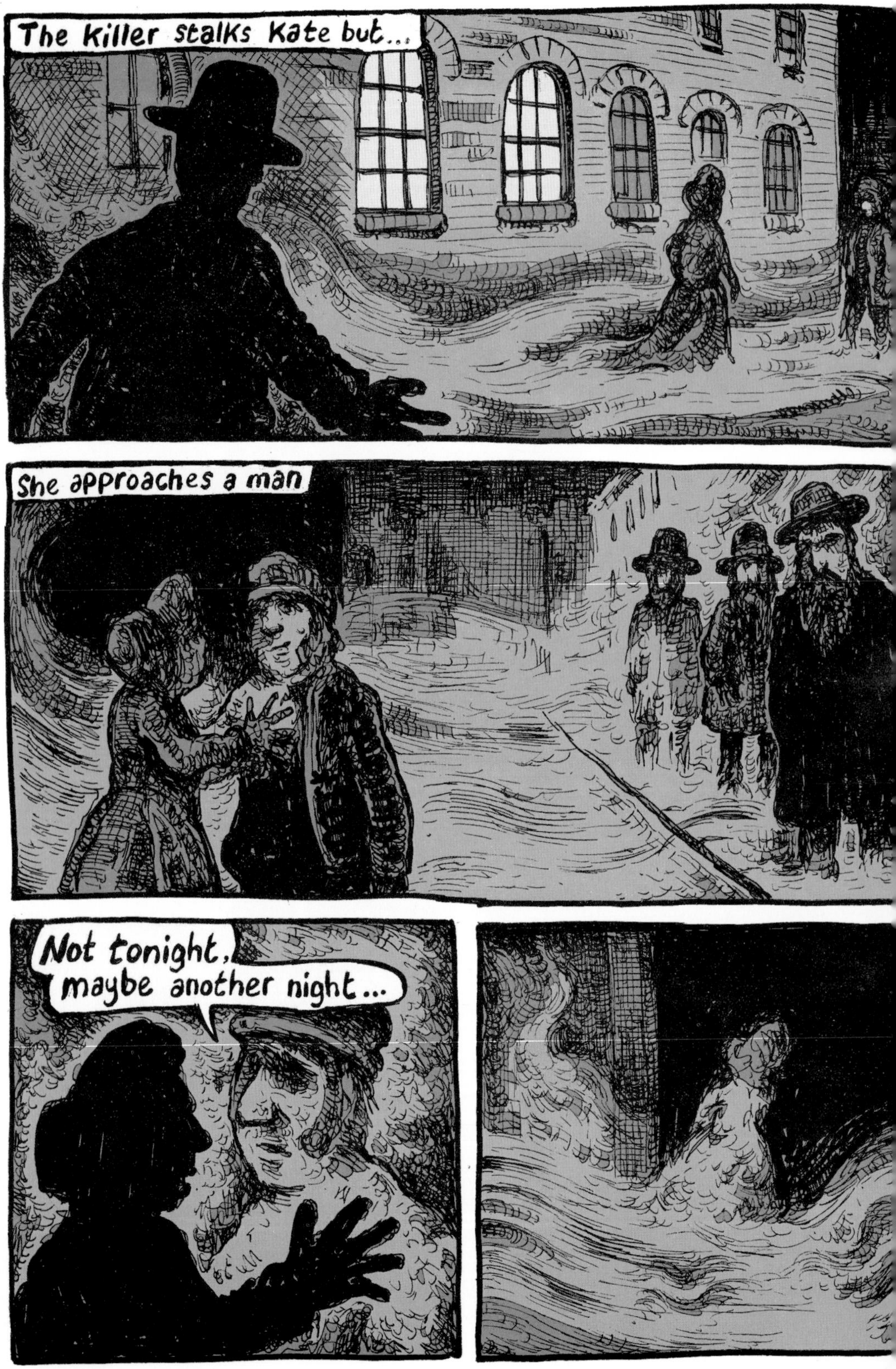
The killer stalks Kate but...
She approaches a man
Not tonight, maybe another night...

As Kate Eddowes turns into Mitre Square, the Killer sees his chance to strike.

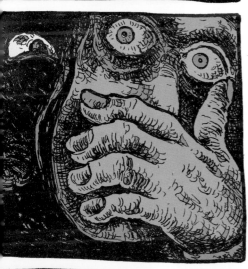

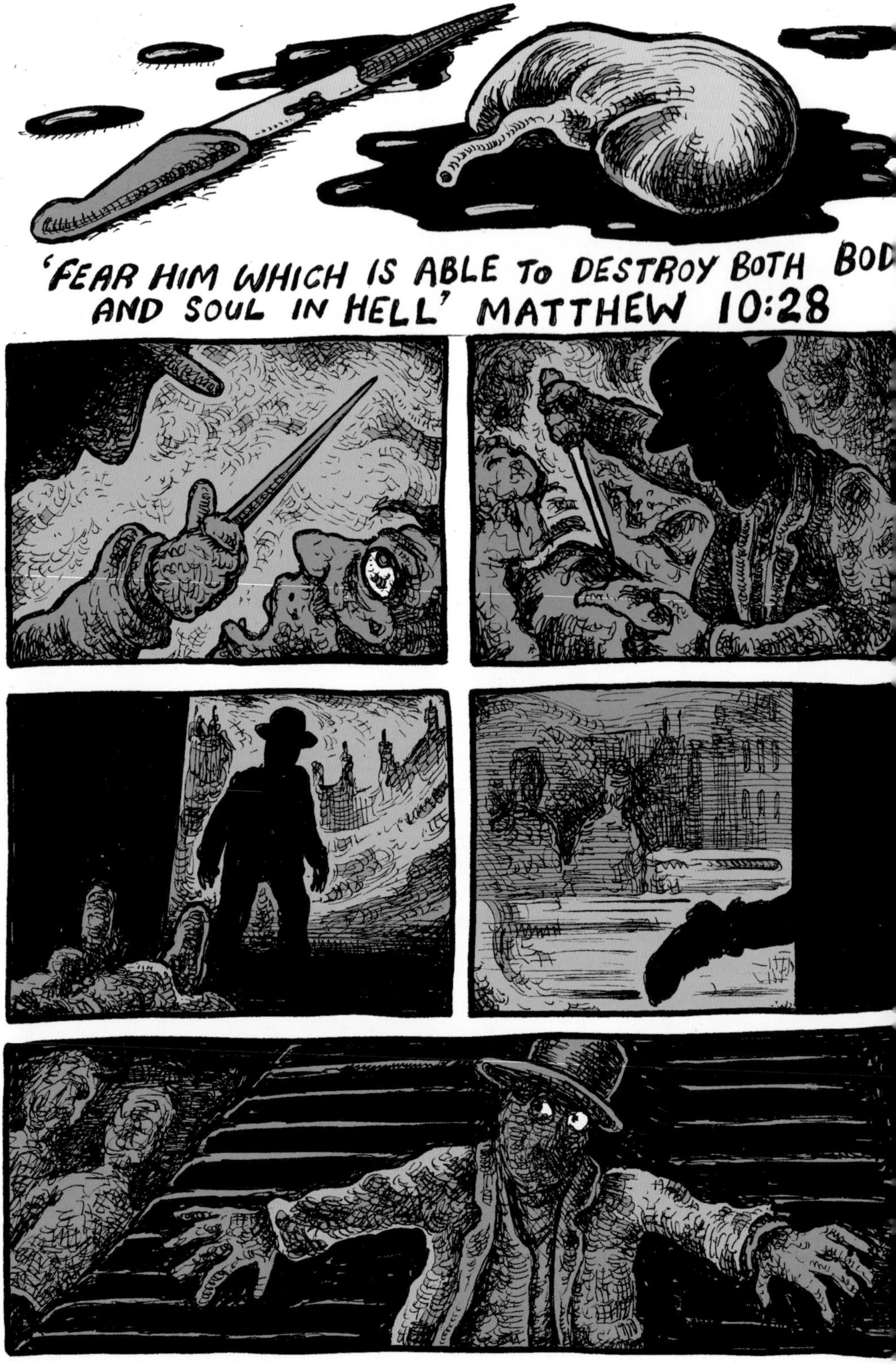
'FEAR HIM WHICH IS ABLE TO DESTROY BOTH BOD
AND SOUL IN HELL' MATTHEW 10:28

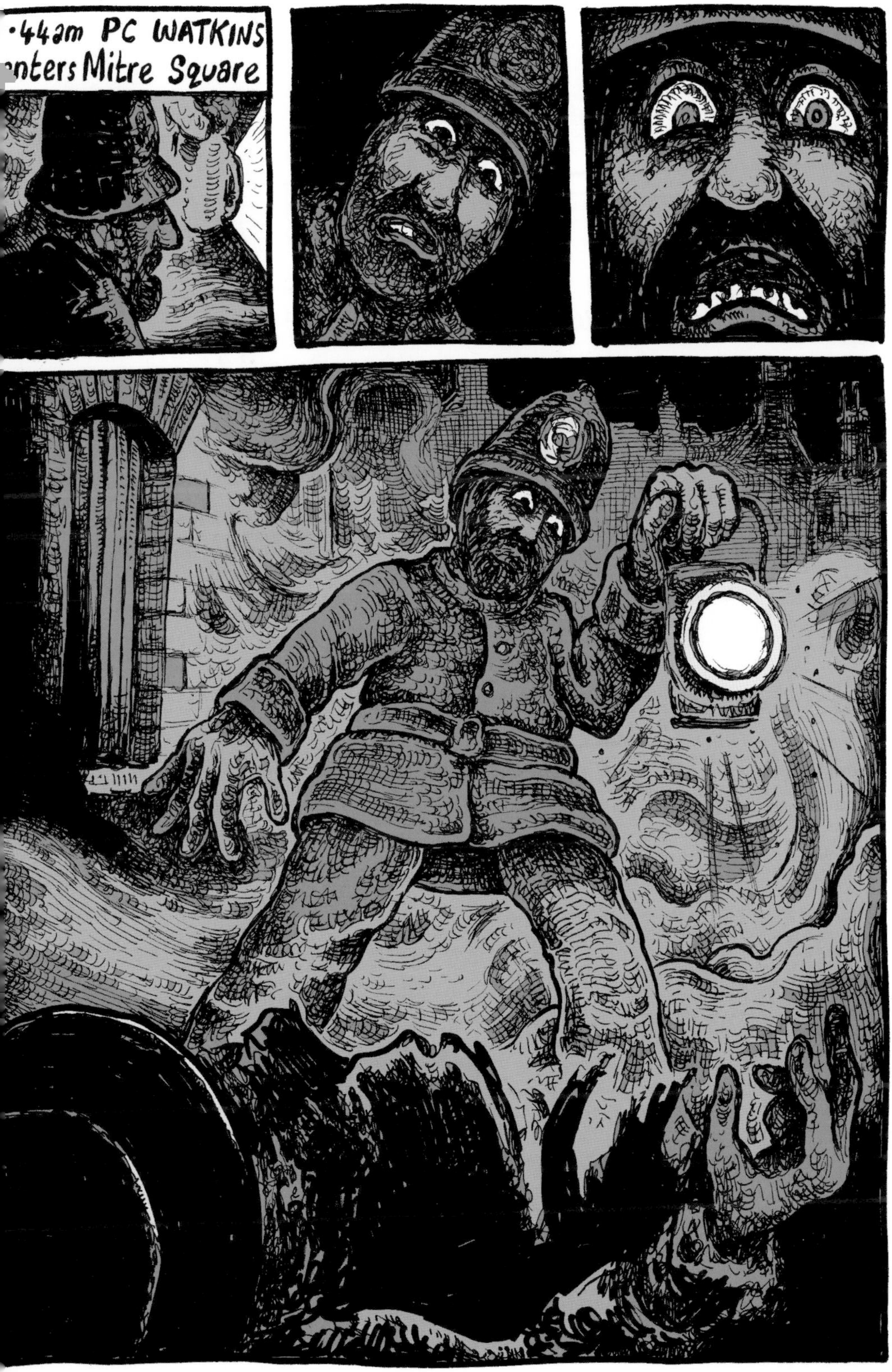
·44am PC WATKINS
nters Mitre Square

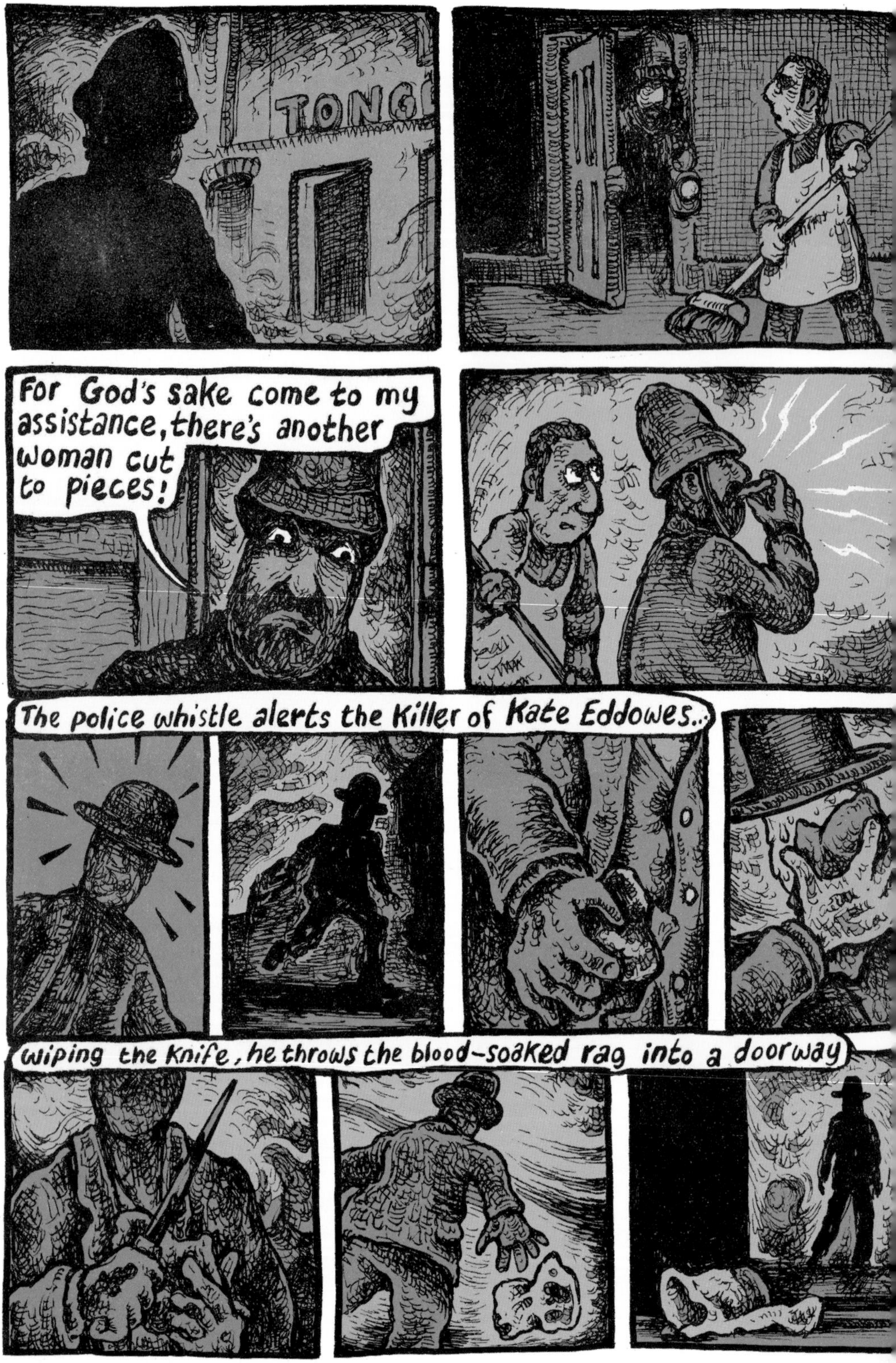
TONG
For God's sake come to my assistance, there's another woman cut to pieces!
The police whistle alerts the Killer of Kate Eddowes...
wiping the Knife, he throws the blood-soaked rag into a doorway

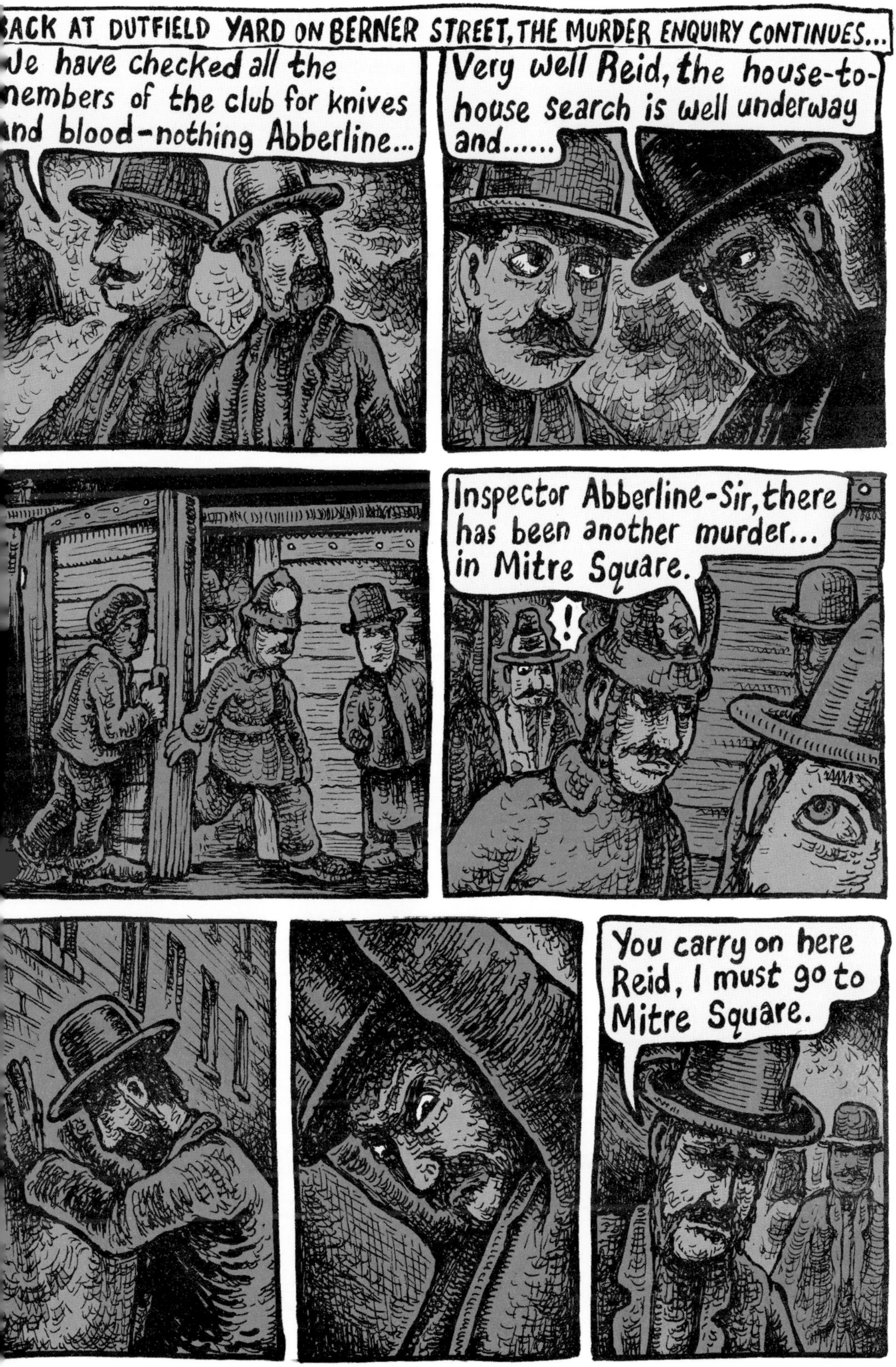
BACK AT DUTFIELD YARD ON BERNER STREET, THE MURDER ENQUIRY CONTINUES...
We have checked all the members of the club for knives and blood-nothing Abberline...
Very well Reid, the house-to-house search is well underway and......
Inspector Abberline-Sir, there has been another murder... in Mitre Square.
!
You carry on here Reid, I must go to Mitre Square.

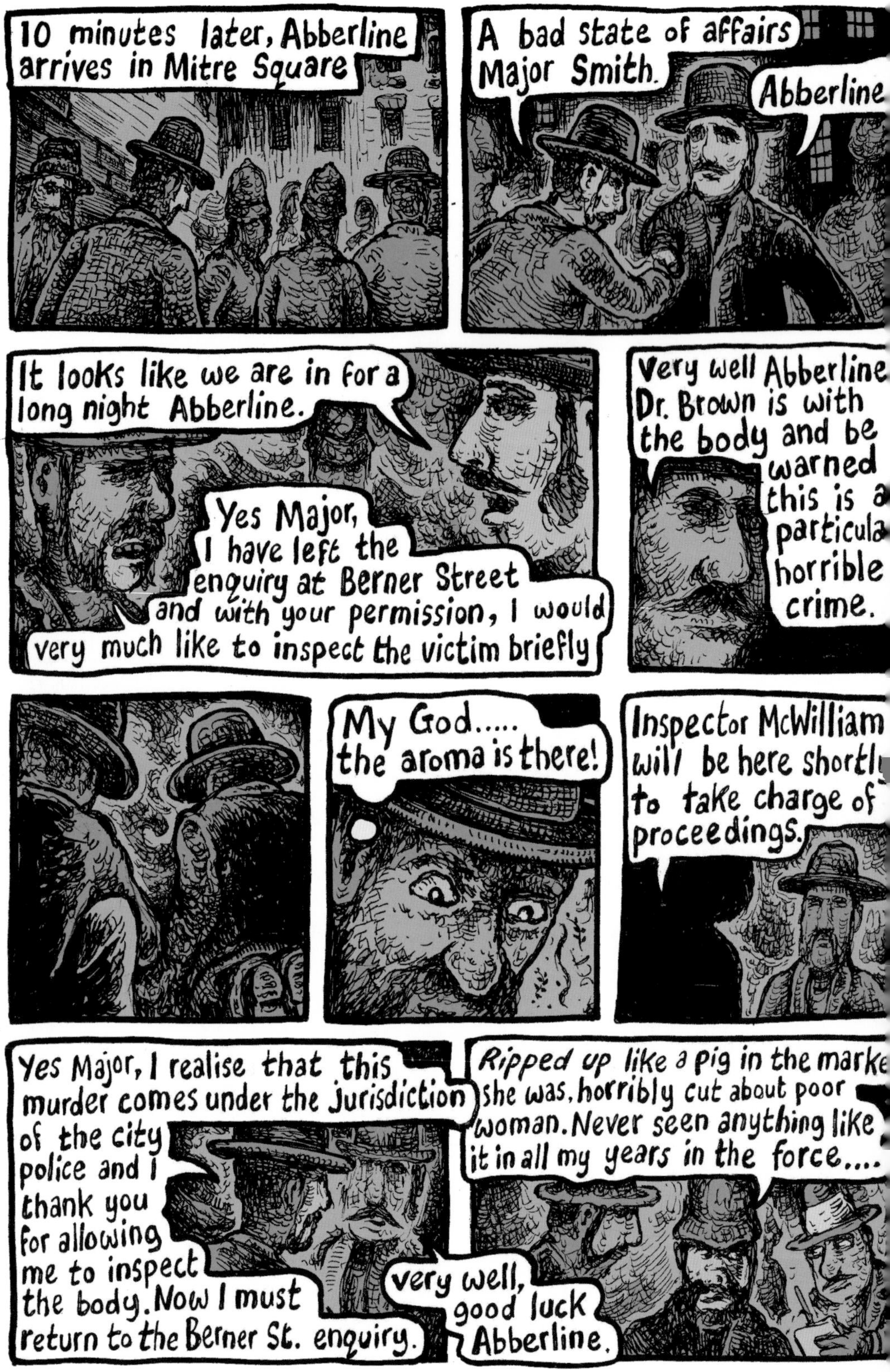
10 minutes later, Abberline arrives in Mitre Square
A bad state of affairs Major Smith.
Abberline
It looks like we are in for a long night Abberline.
Yes Major, I have left the enquiry at Berner Street and with your permission, I would very much like to inspect the victim briefly
Very well Abberline Dr. Brown is with the body and be warned this is a particula horrible crime.
My God..... the aroma is there!
Inspector McWilliam will be here shortl to take charge of proceedings.
Yes Major, I realise that this murder comes under the jurisdiction of the city police and I thank you for allowing me to inspect the body. Now I must return to the Berner St. enquiry.
very well, good luck Abberline.
Ripped up like a pig in the marke she was, horribly cut about poor woman. Never seen anything like it in all my years in the force....

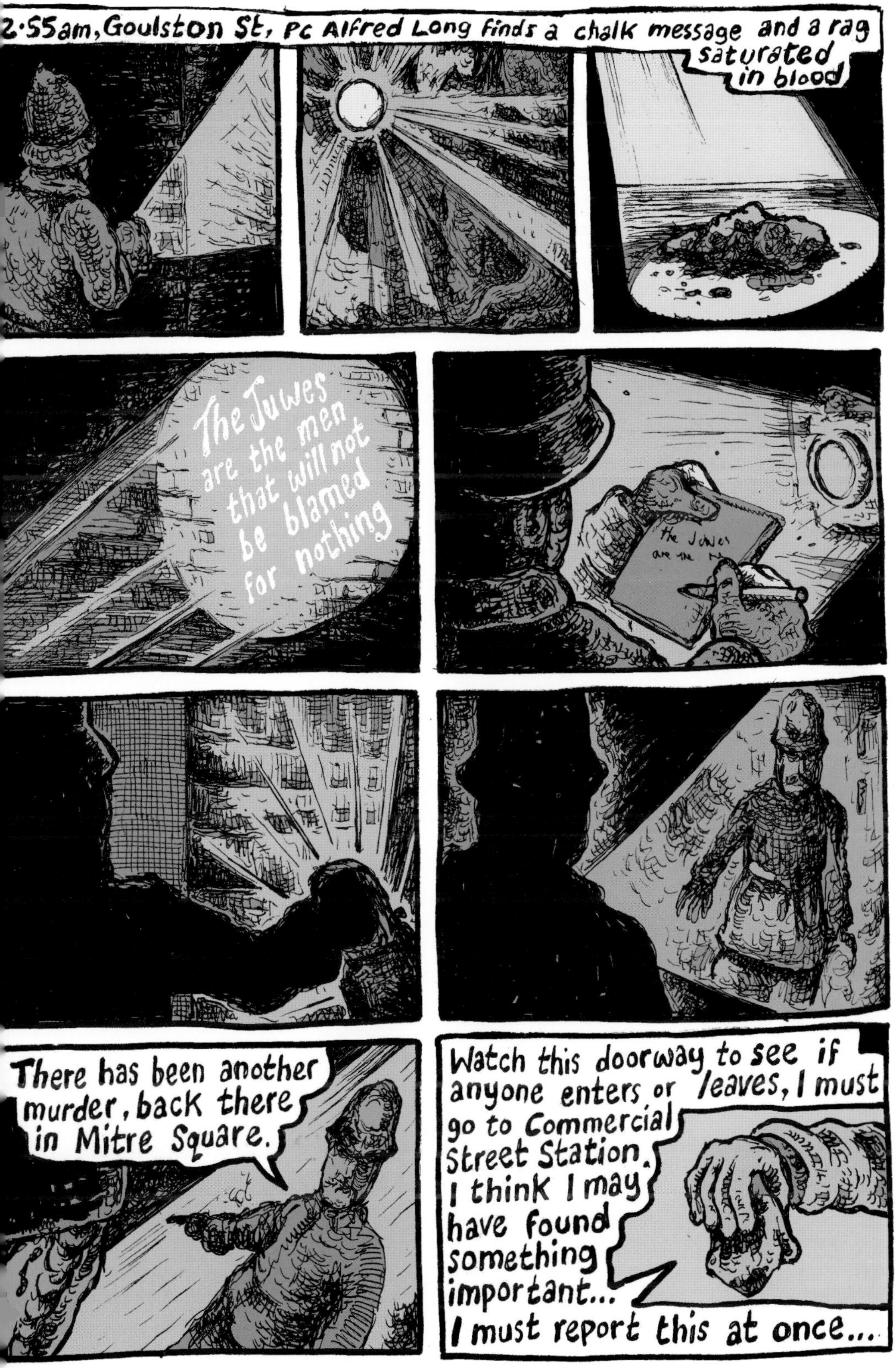
2·55am, Goulston St, Pc Alfred Long finds a chalk message and a rag saturated in blood
The Juwes are the men that will not be blamed for nothing
The Juwes are the
There has been another murder, back there in Mitre Square.
Watch this doorway to see if anyone enters or leaves, I must go to Commercial Street Station. I think I may have found something important...
I must report this at once...

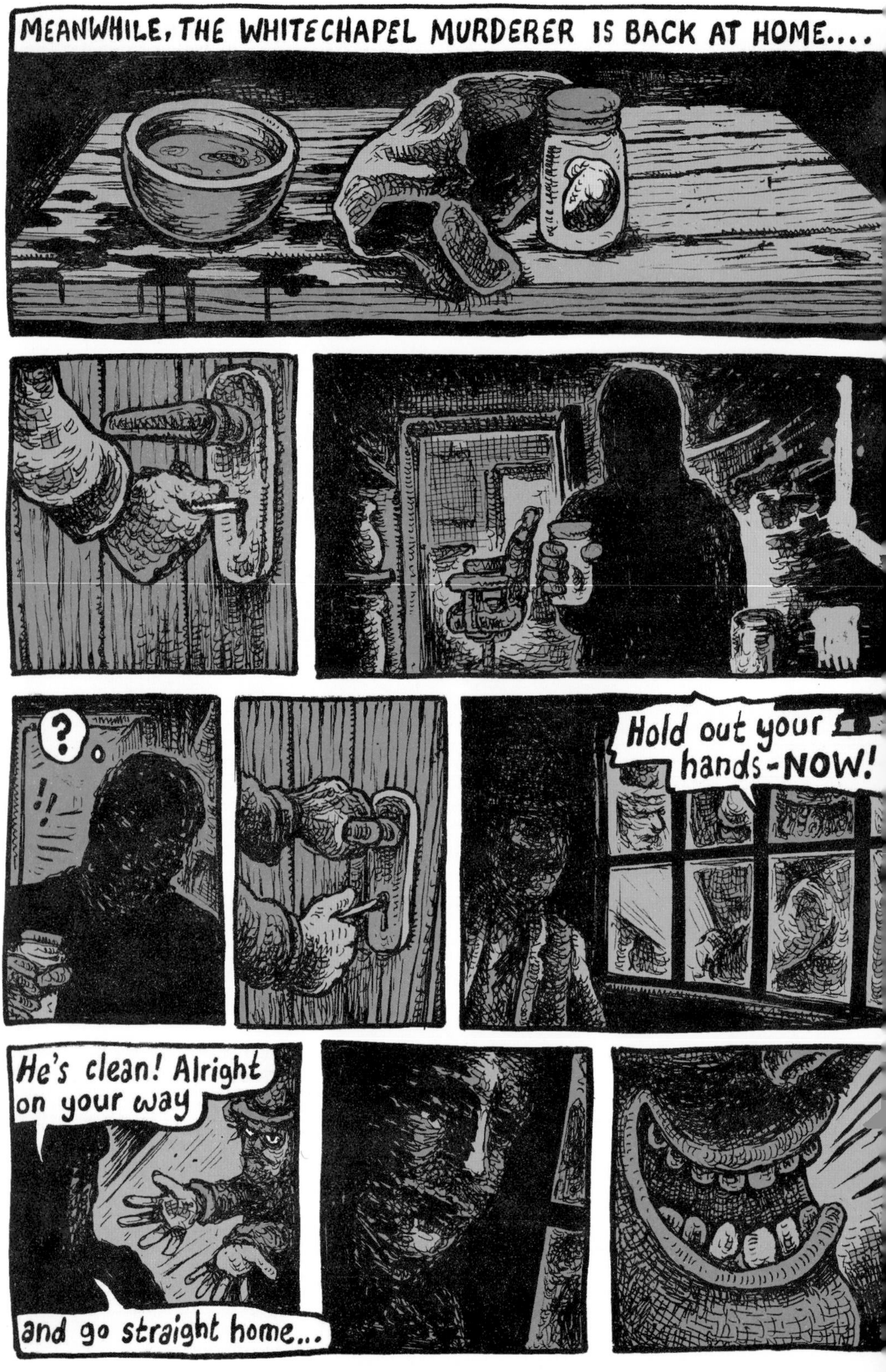
MEANWHILE, THE WHITECHAPEL MURDERER IS BACK AT HOME....
?
!!
Hold out your hands-NOW!
He's clean! Alright on your way
and go straight home...

Back at 108-119 Goulston Street -00am

...and this message was above the bloody piece of apron Superintendent Arnold?

The bloody apron belongs to the woman found in Mitre Square, Sir Charles in City Police jurisdiction.

Thank you Detective Halse!

It is getting light Sir Charles and as you can see, the area is becoming busy.

Yes Arnold, and this area is very much occupied by the Jewish community which is particularly worrying...

The Jewish suspect Leather Apron ...he is still considered as a suspect in some quarters.

Hmm.

And this chalk message naming the Jews could start a riot unless we take immediate action.

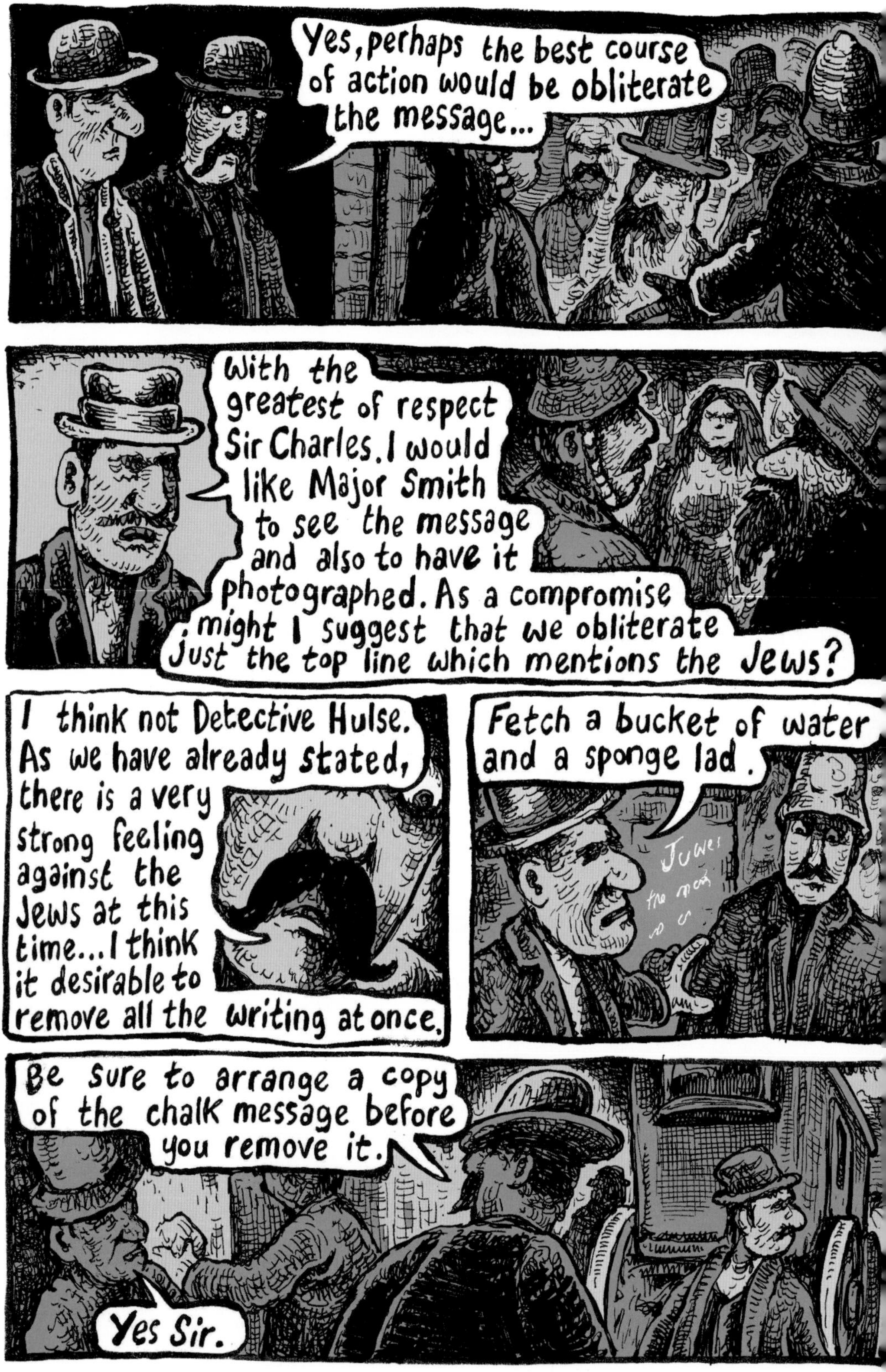
Yes, perhaps the best course of action would be obliterate the message...
With the greatest of respect Sir Charles. I would like Major Smith to see the message and also to have it photographed. As a compromise, might I suggest that we obliterate just the top line which mentions the Jews?
I think not Detective Hulse. As we have already stated, there is a very strong feeling against the Jews at this time... I think it desirable to remove all the writing at once.
Fetch a bucket of water and a sponge lad.
Be sure to arrange a copy of the chalk message before you remove it.
Yes Sir.

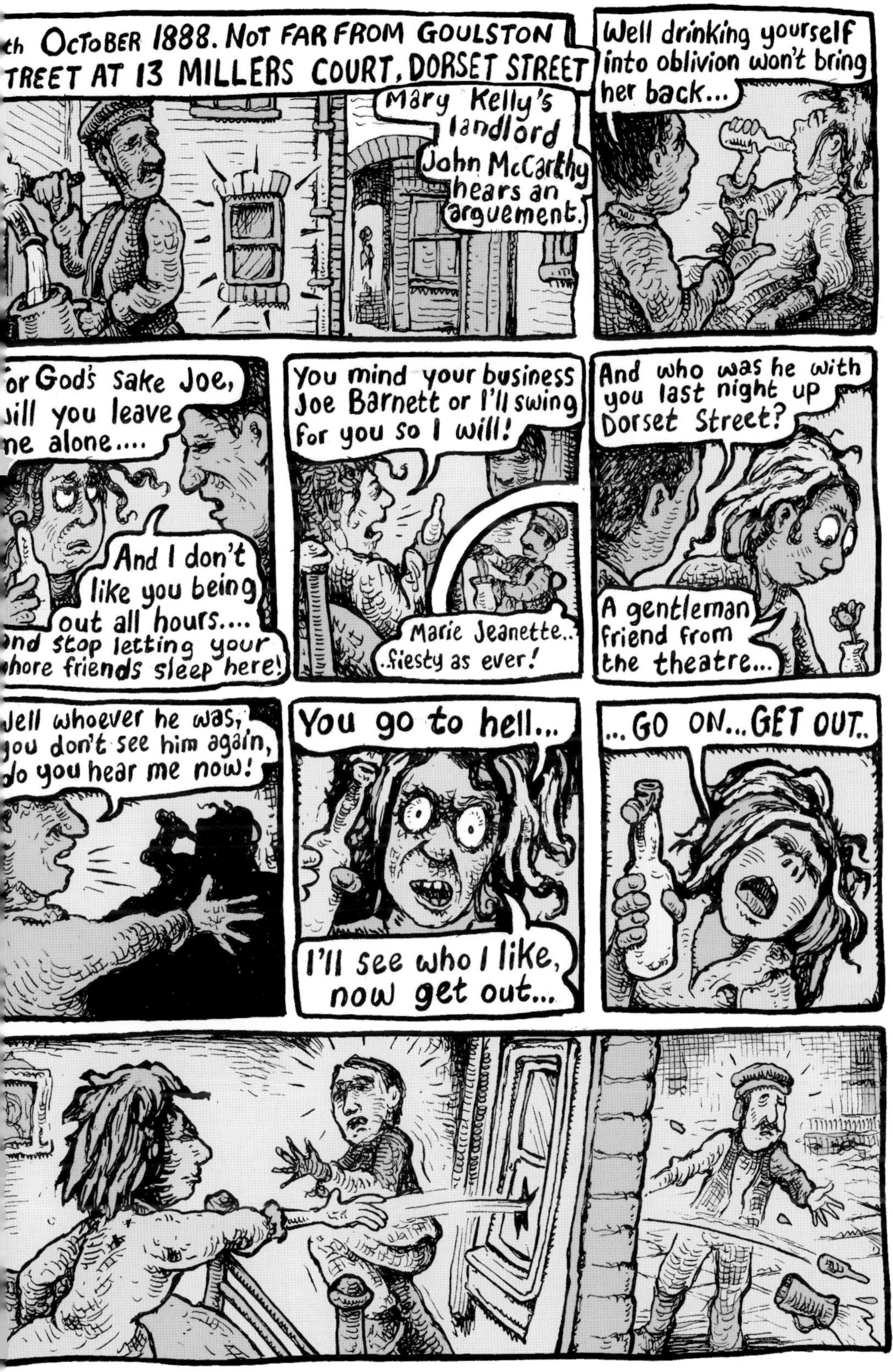
th OCTOBER 1888. NOT FAR FROM GOULSTON
TREET AT 13 MILLERS COURT, DORSET STREET
Mary Kelly's landlord John McCarthy hears an arguement.
Well drinking yourself into oblivion won't bring her back...
or God's sake Joe, will you leave ne alone....
And I don't like you being out all hours.... nd stop letting your hore friends sleep here!
You mind your business Joe Barnett or I'll swing for you so I will!
Marie Jeanette.. ..fiesty as ever!
And who was he with you last night up Dorset Street?
A gentleman friend from the theatre...
Vell whoever he was, you don't see him again, do you hear me now!
You go to hell...
I'll see who I like, now get out...
...GO ON...GET OUT..

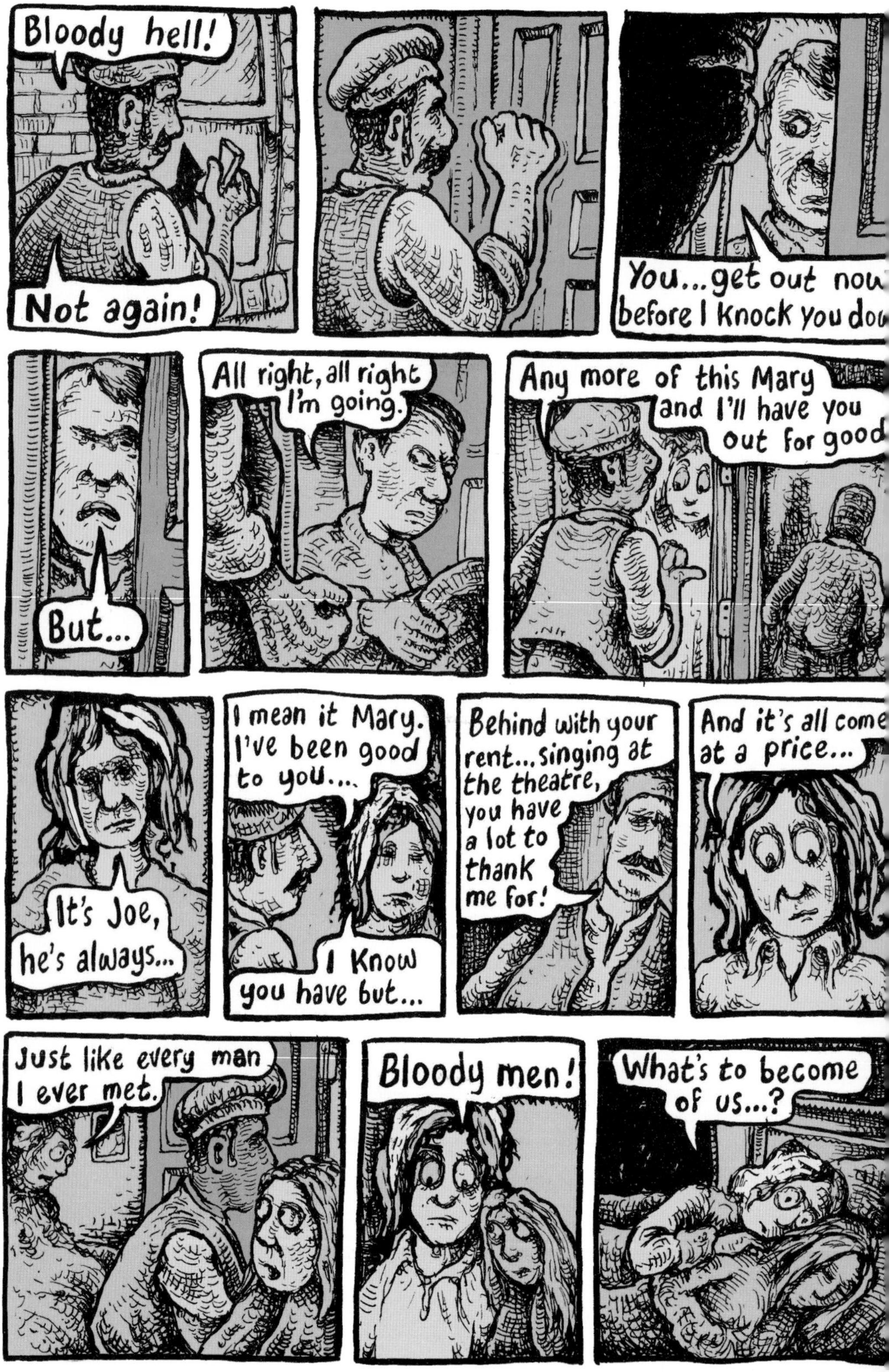

Bloody hell!
Not again!
You...get out now
before I knock you dow
But...
All right, all right
I'm going.
Any more of this Mary
and I'll have you
out for good
It's Joe,
he's always...
I mean it Mary.
I've been good
to you....
I Know
you have but...
Behind with your
rent...singing at
the theatre,
you have
a lot to
thank
me for!
And it's all come
at a price...
Just like every man
I ever met.
Bloody men!
What's to become
of us...?

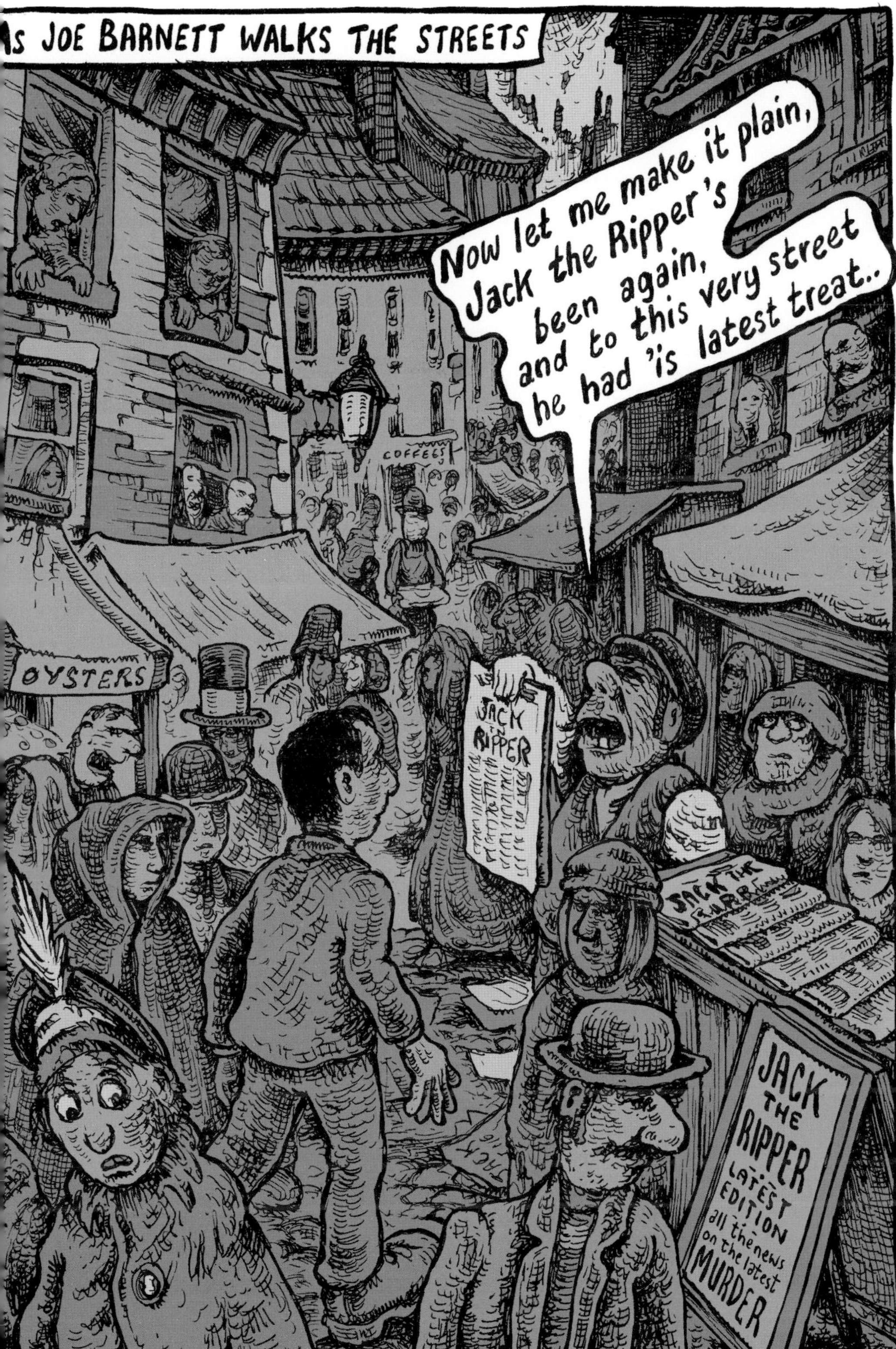
AS JOE BARNETT WALKS THE STREETS
Now let me make it plain, Jack the Ripper's been again, and to this very street he had 'is latest treat..
COFFEES
OYSTERS
JACK THE RIPPER
JACK THE RIPPER
JACK THE RIPPER LATEST EDITION all the news on the latest MURDER

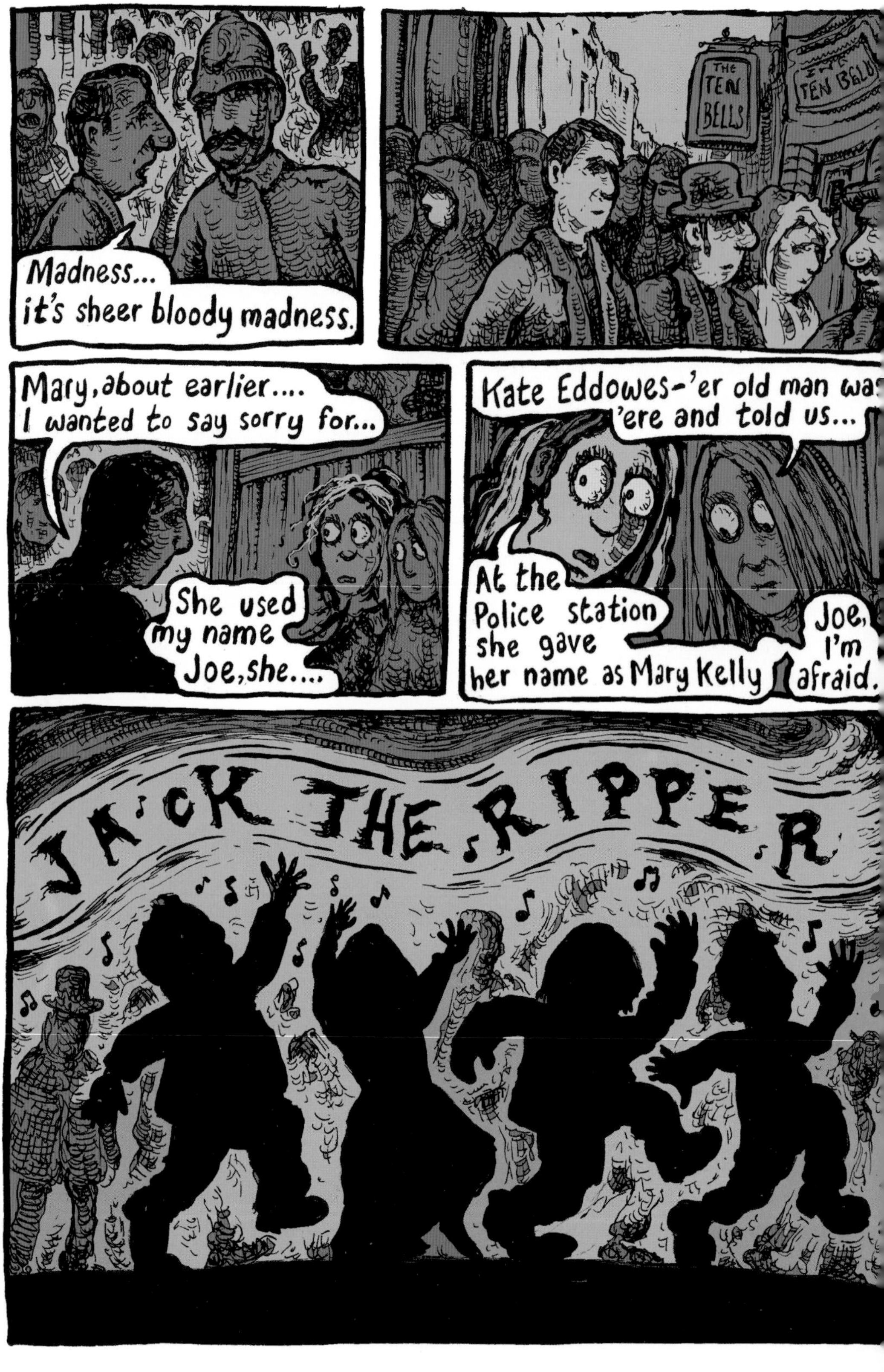
Madness...
it's sheer bloody madness.
THE TEN BELLS
TEN BELLS
Mary, about earlier....
I wanted to say sorry for...
She used my name Joe, she....
Kate Eddowes-'er old man was 'ere and told us...
At the Police station she gave her name as Mary Kelly
Joe, I'm afraid.
JACK THE RIPPER

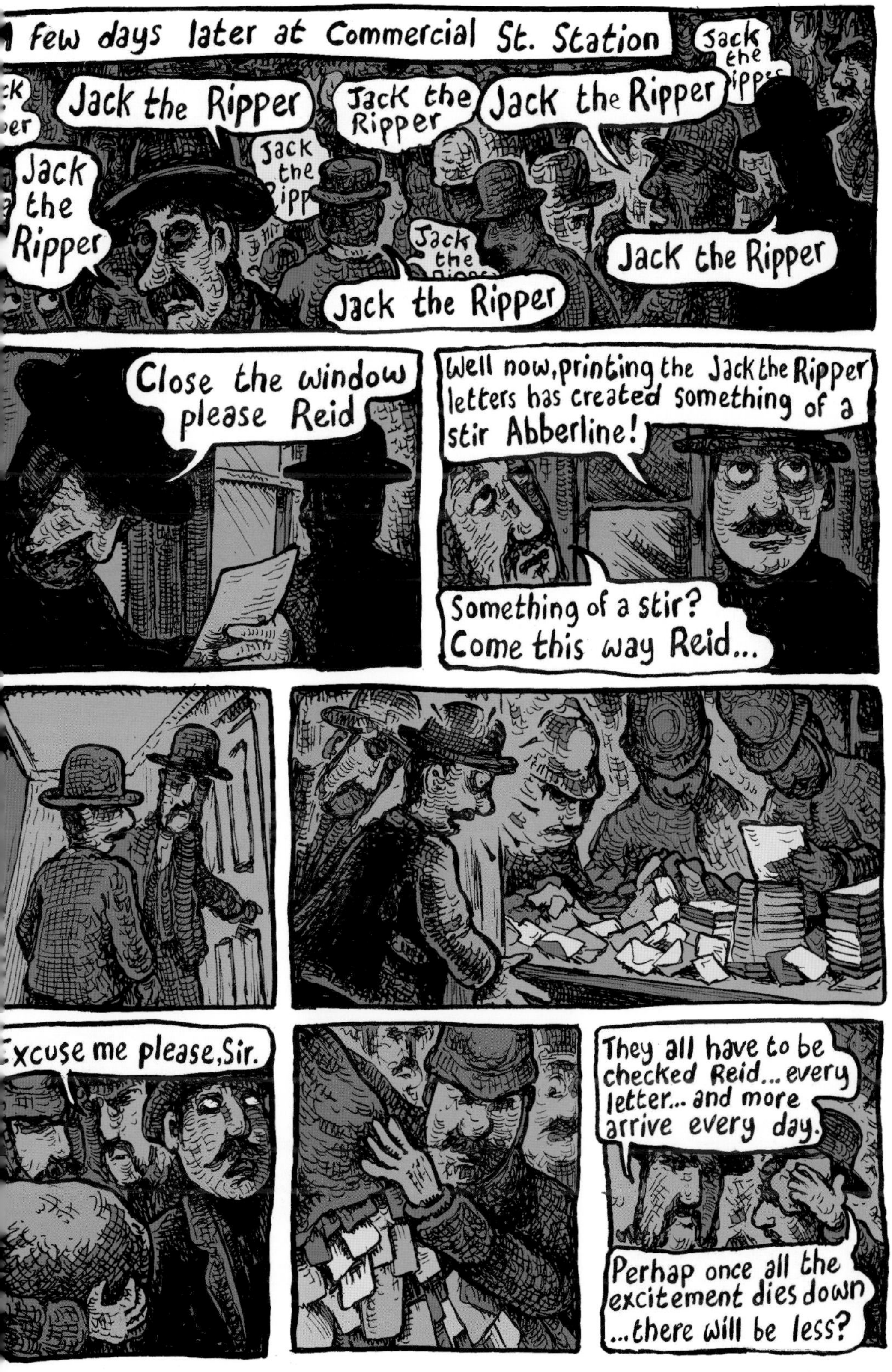
A few days later at Commercial St. Station
Jack the Ripper
Jack the Ripper
Jack the Ripper
Jack the Ripper
Jack the Ripper
Jack the Ripper
Jack the Ripper
Close the window please Reid
Well now, printing the Jack the Ripper letters has created something of a stir Abberline!
Something of a stir? Come this way Reid...
Excuse me please, Sir.
They all have to be checked Reid... every letter... and more arrive every day.
Perhap once all the excitement dies down ...there will be less?

But meanwhile...in the back room of a pub

Well, did you get it...

I'll pay you well... ..nothing will be said, you have my word.

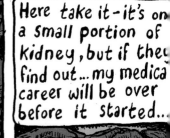

Here take it - it's only a small portion of kidney, but if they find out...my medical career will be over before it started...

Well now...here, take this for your trouble...

STAR NEWSPAPER

From Hell

'From Hell' a very nice touch, even if I say so myself! That should keep the newspaper sales soaring

Come here son..

Where are you taking those letters to be posted?

Gracefield street Sir....

Well be a good lad and post this for me will you?

Yes Sir.

In a backroom at the home of a Killer

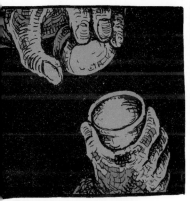

Why... Why?

He walks the Whitechapel Rd

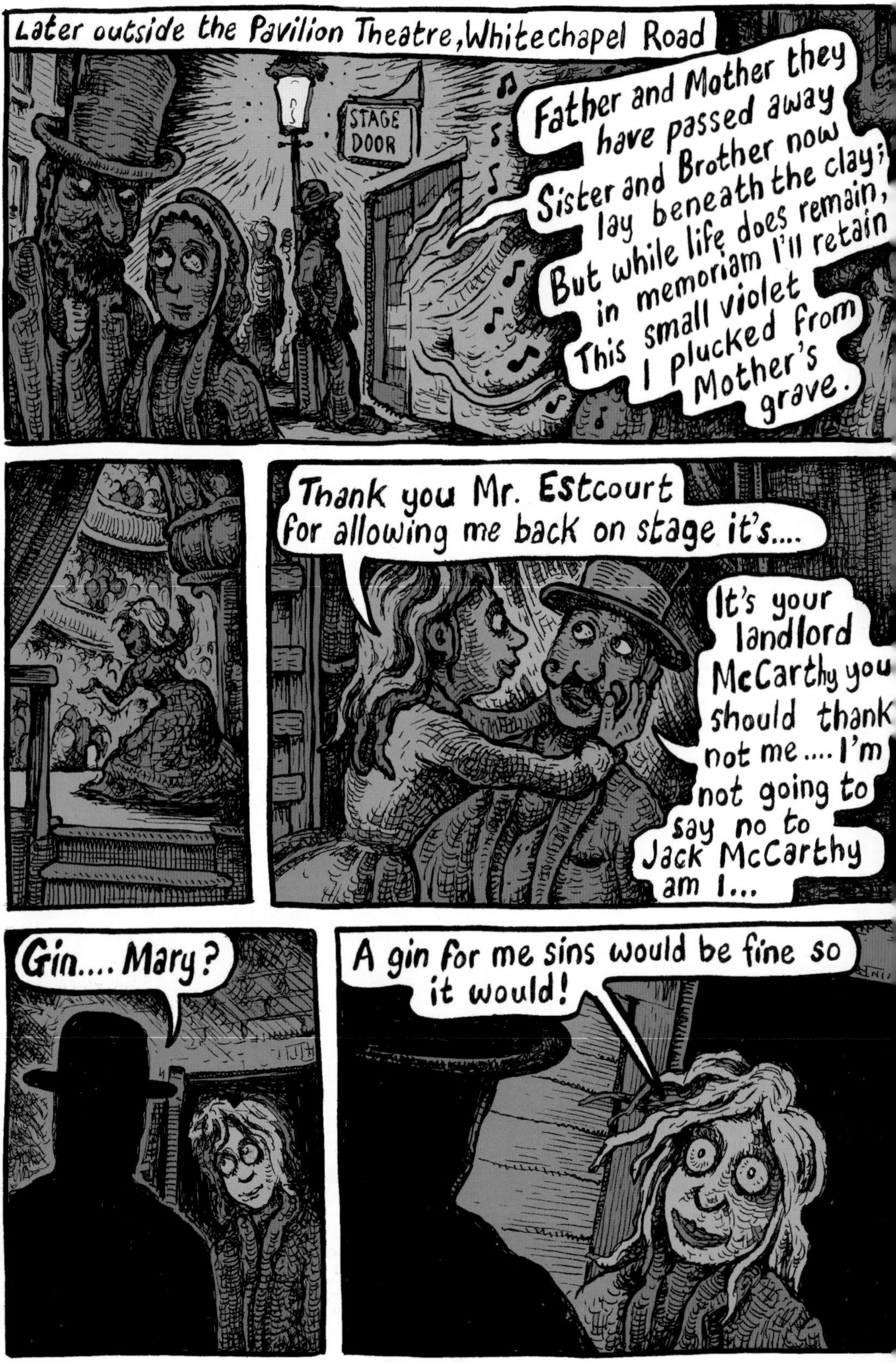
Later outside the Pavilion Theatre, Whitechapel Road
STAGE DOOR
Father and Mother they have passed away Sister and Brother now lay beneath the clay; But while life does remain, in memoriam I'll retain This small violet I plucked from Mother's grave.
Thank you Mr. Estcourt for allowing me back on stage it's....
It's your landlord McCarthy you should thank not me.... I'm not going to say no to Jack McCarthy am I...
Gin.... Mary?
A gin for me sins would be fine so it would!

A short walk to The Frying Pan

You're a quiet one all right, hardly say a word do you?

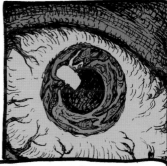

Only the one drink now, my old man will be waiting and...

It's beautiful.

For you... Mary Kelly

No, thank you but...no!

We go now Mary...

lease take it ack...please...

MARY! I warned you not to see him...

Joe Barnett loses control

I'll kill him...I'll kill him..

The killer runs into Itchy Park

...Where the East End homless sleep...

BRONISLAW ZAPOLSKI
BORN POLAND
THE PAST IS NEVER DEAD

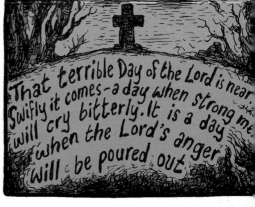

That terrible Day of the Lord is near. Swiftly it comes—a day when strong men will cry bitterly. It is a day when the Lord's anger will be poured out

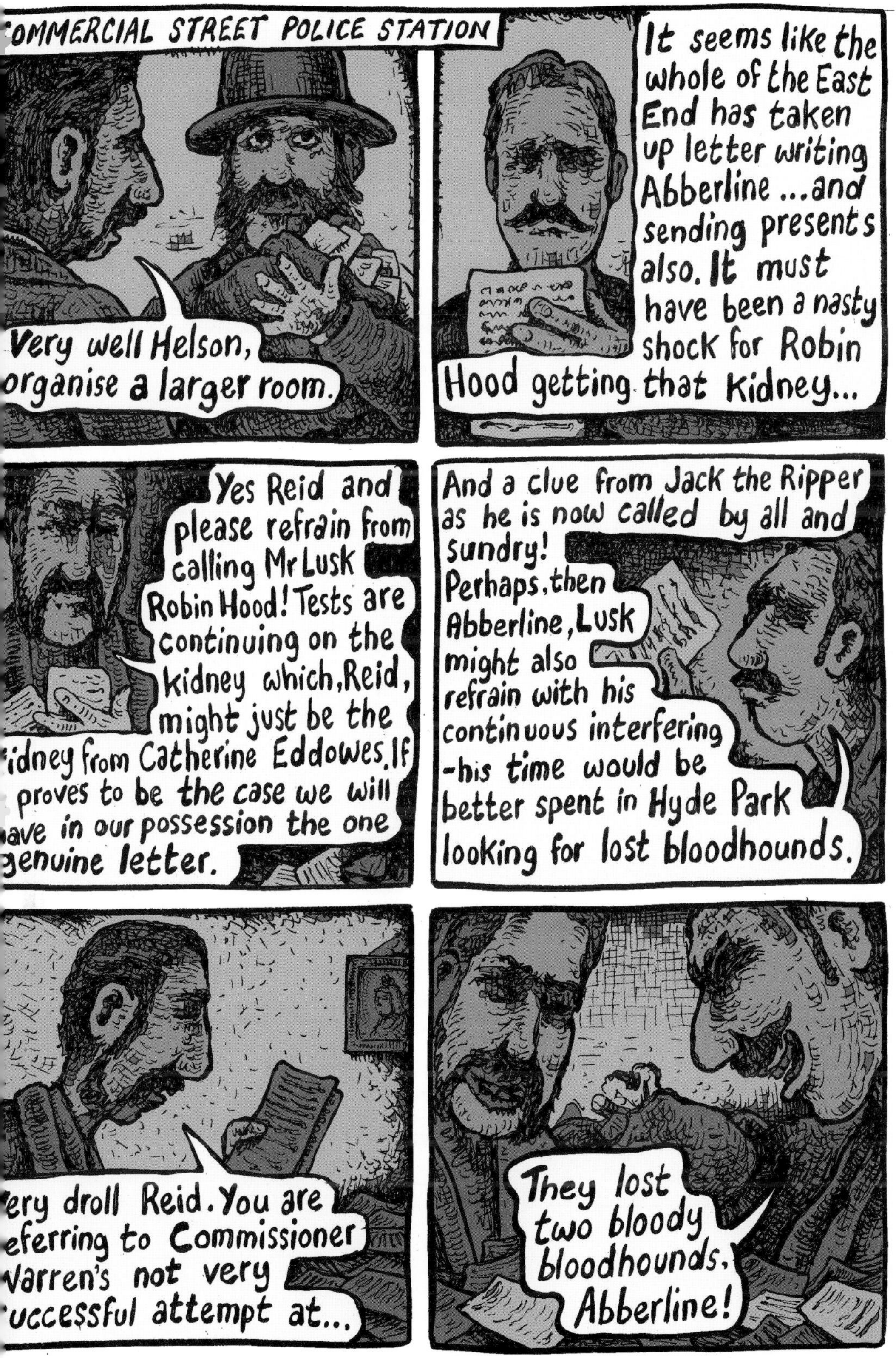
OMMERCIAL STREET POLICE STATION
Very well Helson, organise a larger room.
It seems like the whole of the East End has taken up letter writing Abberline ...and sending presents also. It must have been a nasty shock for Robin Hood getting that Kidney...
Yes Reid and please refrain from calling Mr Lusk Robin Hood! Tests are continuing on the kidney which, Reid, might just be the idney from Catherine Eddowes. If proves to be the case we will ave in our possession the one genuine letter.
And a clue from Jack the Ripper as he is now called by all and sundry!
Perhaps, then Abberline, Lusk might also refrain with his continuous interfering -his time would be better spent in Hyde Park looking for lost bloodhounds.
ery droll Reid. You are eferring to Commissioner Varren's not very uccessful attempt at...
They lost two bloody bloodhounds, Abberline!

JUST DOWN COMMERCIAL STREET AT MILLERS COURT

And I'll tell you something else Joe, you can get out so you can... and this time don't come back! Take your things and leave us be...

Very well...But I'll be back. You need me more than you realise Mary... or should I call you Marie Jeannette to fit in with your fancy theatre friends..

You forgot your black coat Joe, you might need it later on!

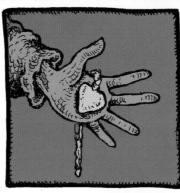

NEXT MORNING

I'm right hungry Mary -we needs to eat!

I haven't any money

but I'll be back shortly...

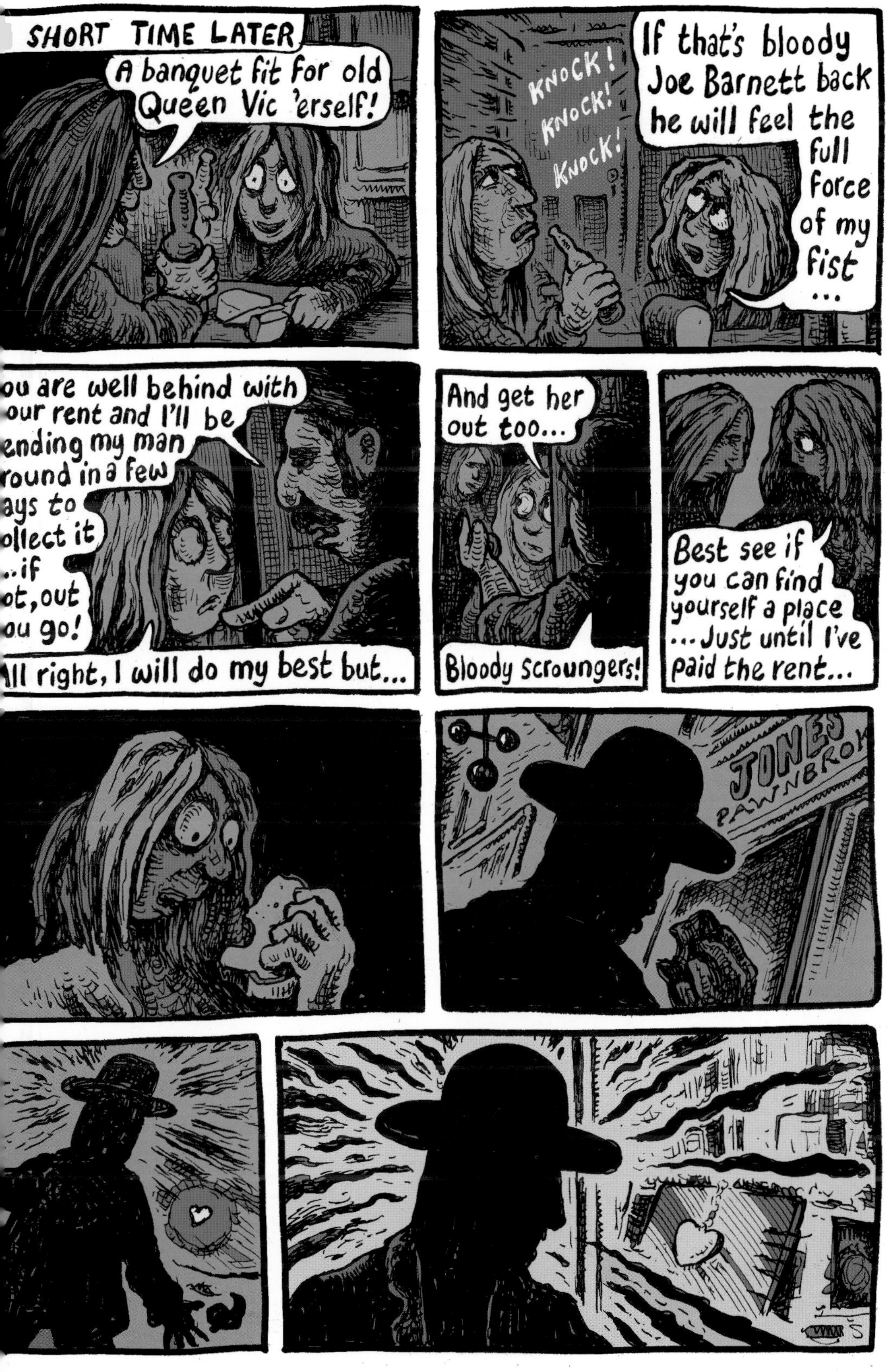
SHORT TIME LATER
A banquet fit for old Queen Vic 'erself!
KNOCK! KNOCK! KNOCK!
If that's bloody Joe Barnett back he will feel the full force of my fist ...
ou are well behind with our rent and I'll be ending my man round in a few ays to ollect it ..if ot, out ou go!
ll right, I will do my best but...
And get her out too...
Bloody scroungers!
Best see if you can find yourself a place ... Just until I've paid the rent...
JONES
PAWNBROK

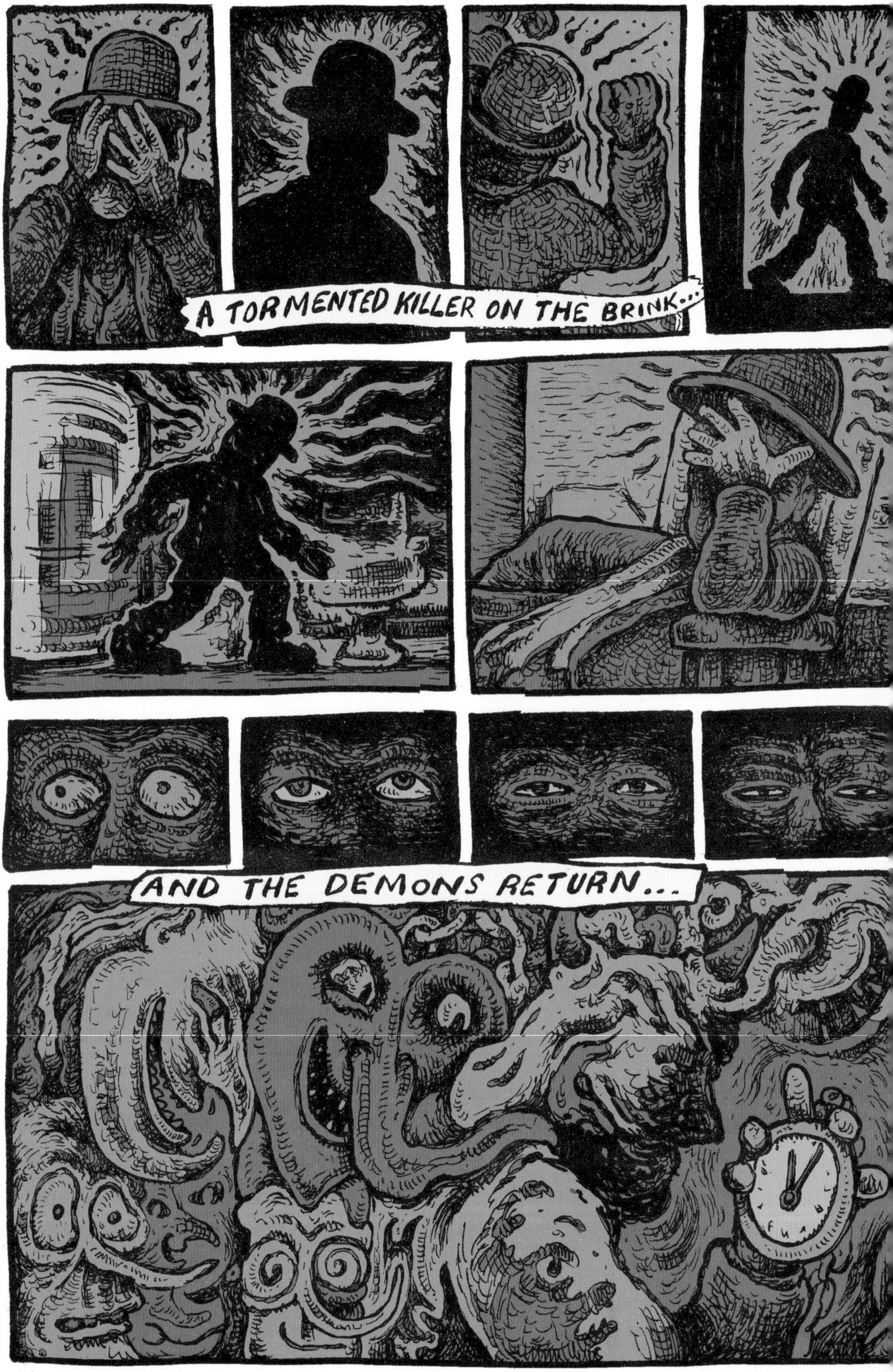
A TORMENTED KILLER ON THE BRINK...
AND THE DEMONS RETURN...

HE KNOWS WHAT HE MUST DO...

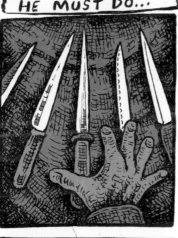

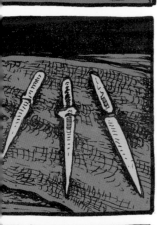
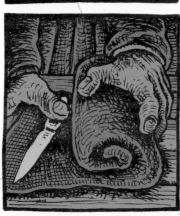

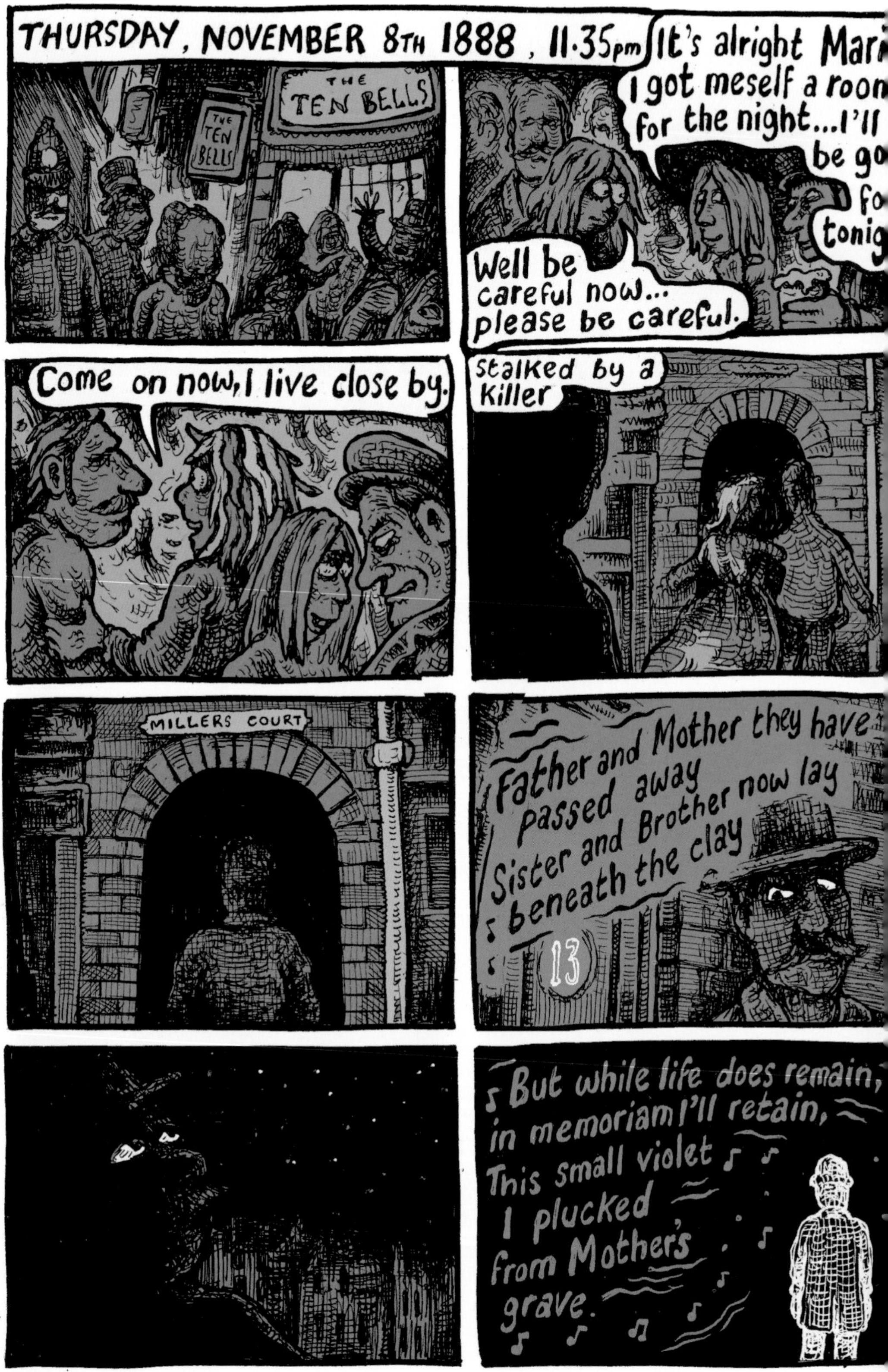
THURSDAY, NOVEMBER 8TH 1888, 11.35pm
THE TEN BELLS
THE TEN BELLS
It's alright Mar
I got meself a roon
for the night...I'll
be go
fo
tonig
Well be careful now... please be careful.
Come on now, I live close by.
stalked by a killer
MILLERS COURT
Father and Mother they have passed away
Sister and Brother now lay beneath the clay
13
But while life does remain,
in memoriam I'll retain,
This small violet
I plucked
from Mother's grave.

FRIDAY, NOVEMBER 9TH 1888, 2.00am

Hutchinson can you lend me sixpence?

Sorry Mary, I've spent all me money going down Romford way so I'm...

Mary Jane Kelly very drunk, sees an old friend

Well I need to find some money...goodnight old cock!

ha-ha-ha

George Hutchinson gets a good look at the killer.

MILLERS COURT

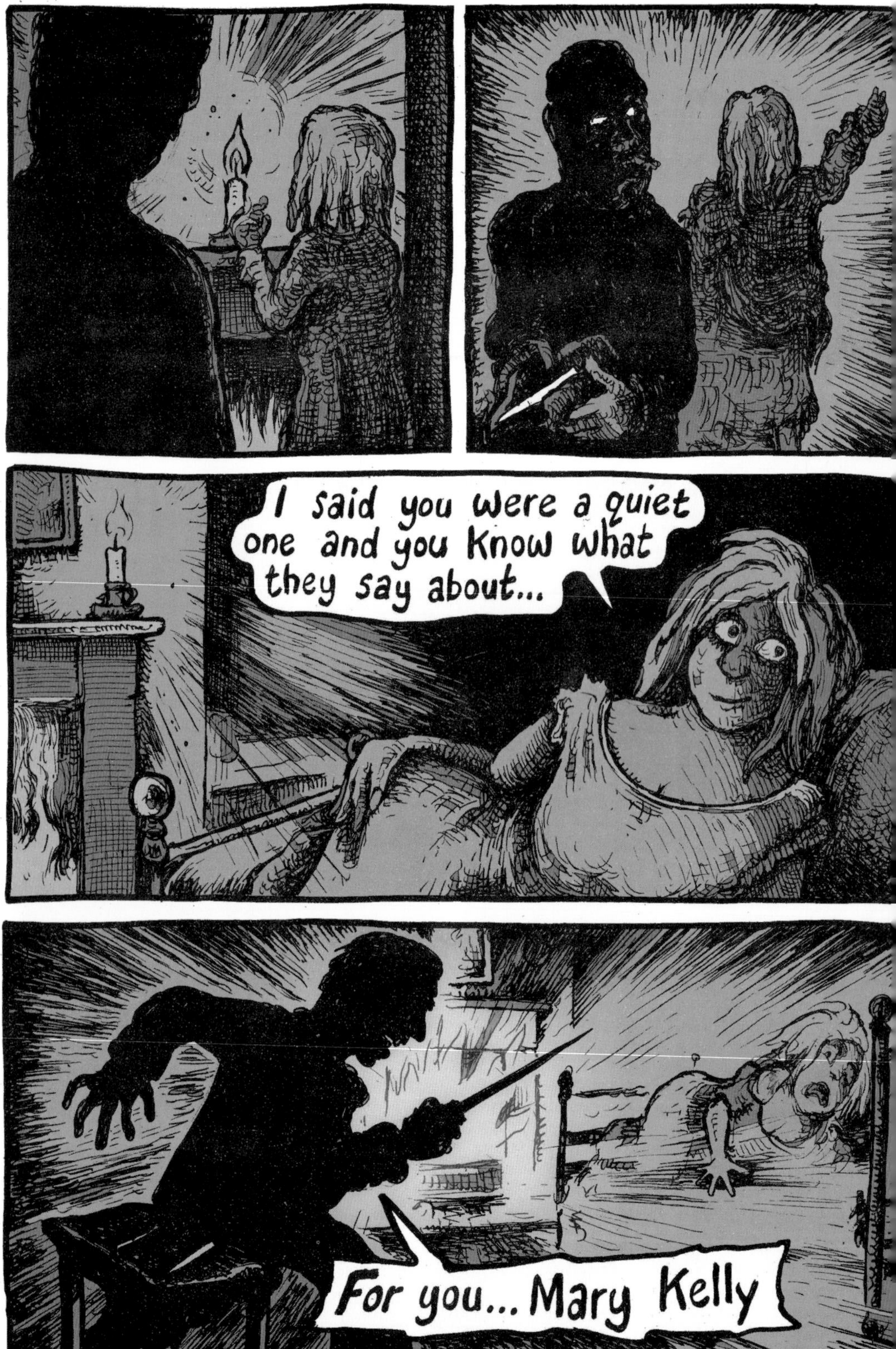
I said you were a quiet one and you know what they say about...
For you... Mary Kelly

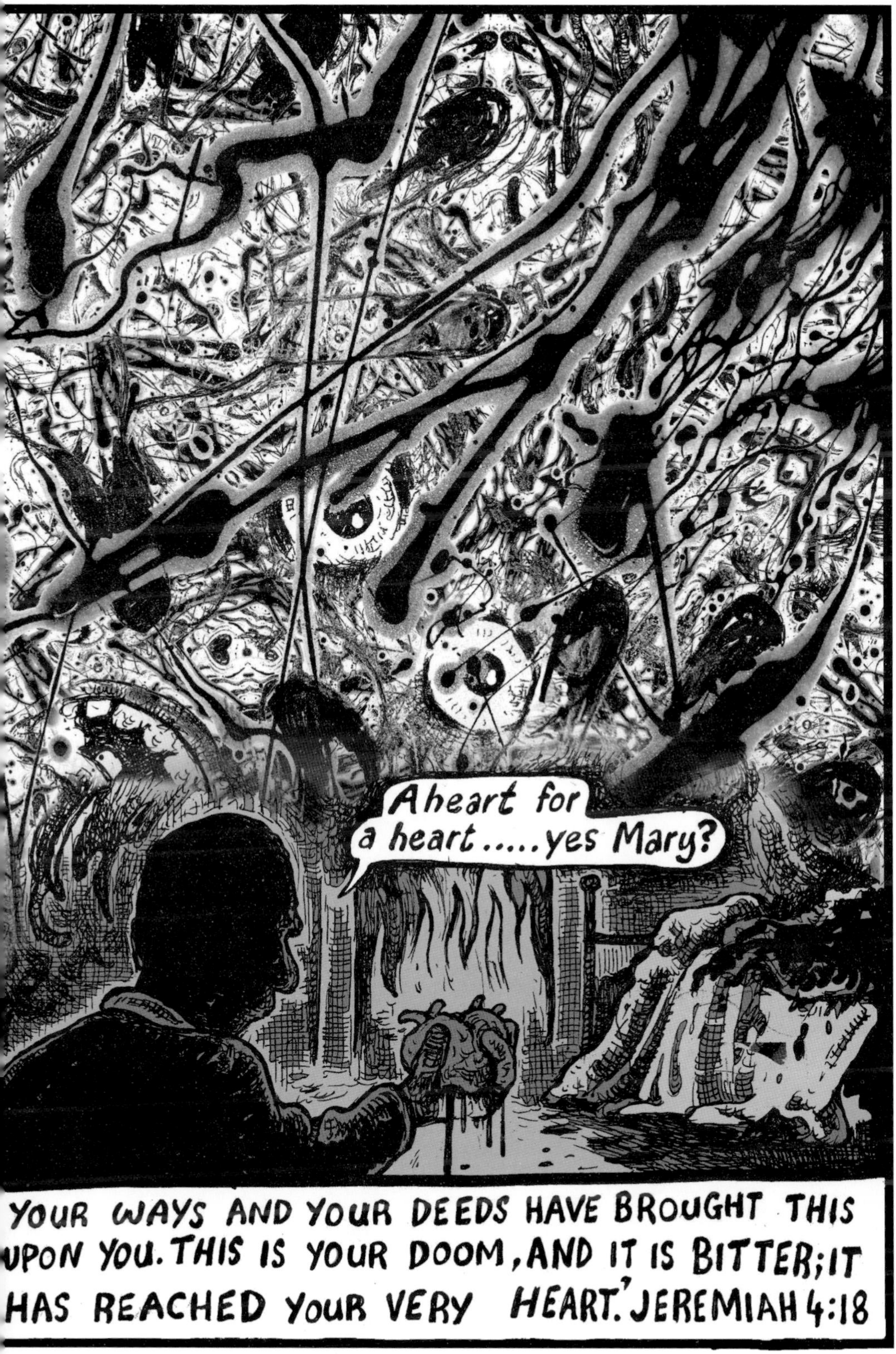
A heart for a heart.....yes Mary?
YOUR WAYS AND YOUR DEEDS HAVE BROUGHT THIS UPON YOU. THIS IS YOUR DOOM, AND IT IS BITTER; IT HAS REACHED YOUR VERY HEART.' JEREMIAH 4:18

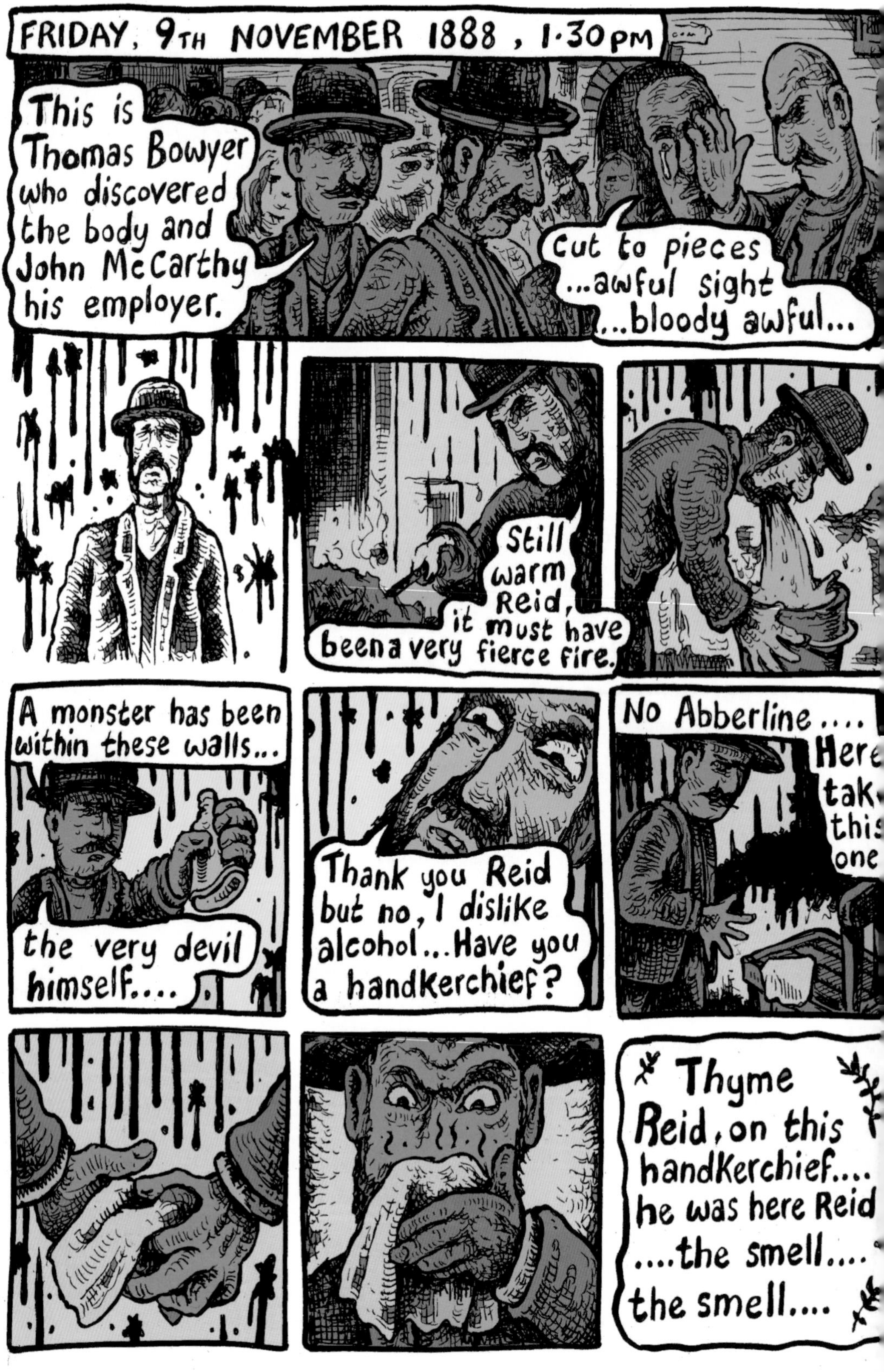
FRIDAY, 9TH NOVEMBER 1888, 1·30PM
This is Thomas Bowyer who discovered the body and John McCarthy his employer.
Cut to pieces ...awful sight ...bloody awful...
Still warm Reid, it must have been a very fierce fire.
A monster has been within these walls...
the very devil himself....
Thank you Reid but no, I dislike alcohol...Have you a handkerchief?
No Abberline....
Here take this one
Thyme Reid, on this handkerchief.... he was here Reid ....the smell.... the smell....

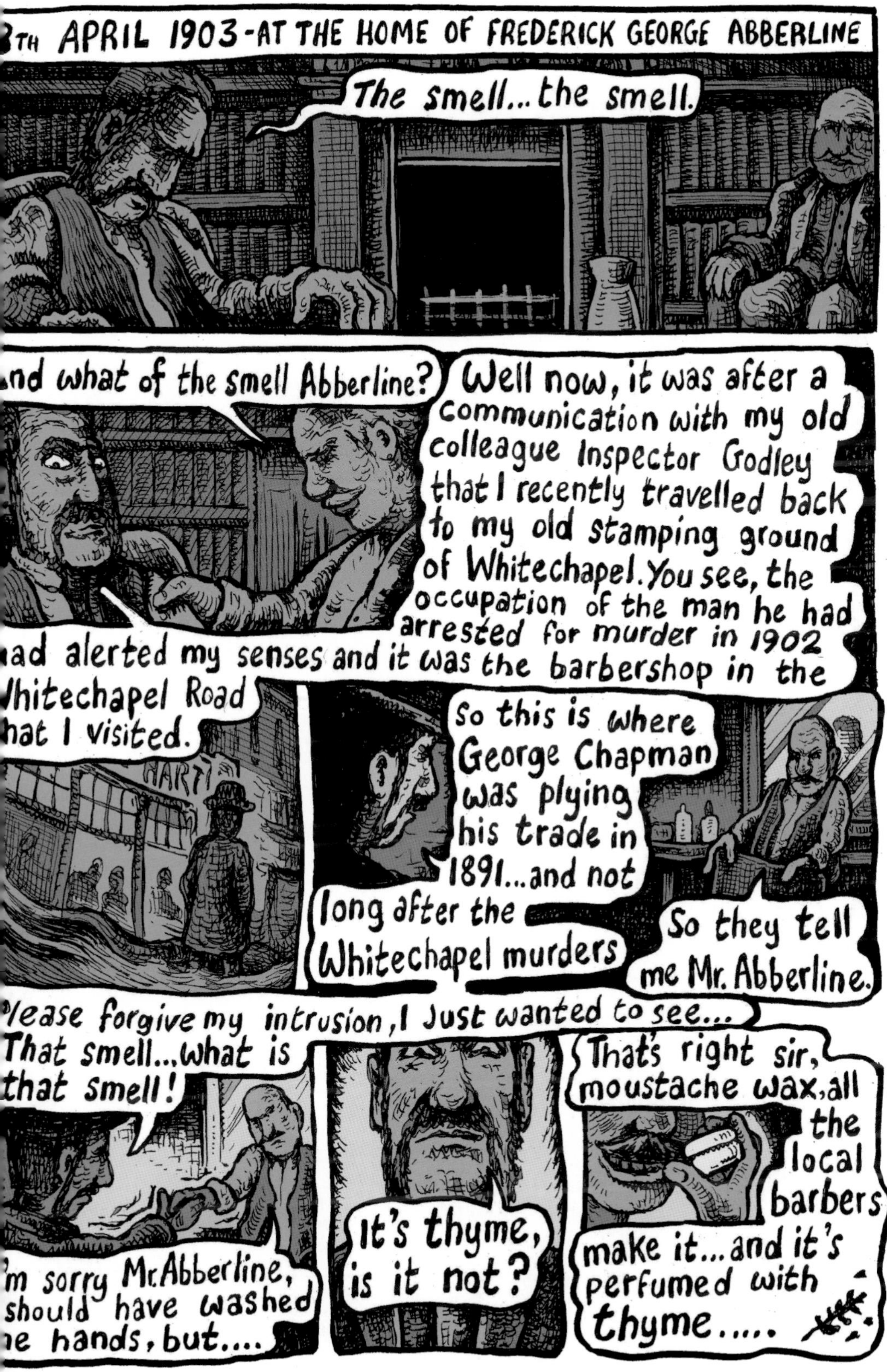

3TH APRIL 1903 - AT THE HOME OF FREDERICK GEORGE ABBERLINE
The smell... the smell.
nd what of the smell Abberline?
Well now, it was after a communication with my old colleague Inspector Godley that I recently travelled back to my old stamping ground of Whitechapel. You see, the occupation of the man he had arrested for murder in 1902 ad alerted my senses and it was the barbershop in the Vhitechapel Road hat I visited.
HARTI
So this is where George Chapman was plying his trade in 1891...and not long after the Whitechapel murders
So they tell me Mr. Abberline.
Please forgive my intrusion, I just wanted to see...
That smell...what is that smell!
'm sorry Mr. Abberline, should have washed ne hands, but....
It's thyme, is it not?
That's right sir, moustache wax, all the local barbers make it...and it's perfumed with thyme.....

Also from The History Press

JACK THE RIPPER

Find these titles and more at
www.thehistorypress.co.uk